ALWAYS THINK BIG

Jim "MATTRESS MACK" McIngvale
with *Thomas N. Duening* & *John M. Ivancevich*

Dearborn™
Trade Publishing
A **Kaplan Professional** Company

This publication is designed to provide accurate and authoritative information in regard to the subject matter covered. It is sold with the understanding that the publisher is not engaged in rendering legal, accounting, or other professional service. If legal advice or other expert assistance is required, the services of a competent professional person should be sought.

Acquisitions Editor: Mary B. Good
Senior Project Editor: Trey Thoelcke
Interior Design: Lucy Jenkins
Cover Design: Design Alliance, Inc.
Typesetting: Elizabeth Pitts

Published by Dearborn Trade Publishing, a Kaplan Professional Company

Printed in the United States of America

04 05 06 10 9 8 7 6 5 4 3 2

Library of Congress Cataloging-in-Publication Data

McIngvale, Jim.
    Always think big : how Mattress Mack's uncompromising attitude built the biggest single retail store in America / Jim McIngvale, Thomas N. Duening, John M. Ivancevich.
        p.   cm.
    ISBN 0-7931-5375-1
    1. Success in business. 2. Gallery Furniture (Houston, Tex.) I. Title: How Mattress Mack's uncompromising attitude built the biggest single retail store in America. II. Duening, Thomas N. III. Ivancevich, John M. IV. Title.
    HF5386 .M193   2002
    658—dc21
                                                                    2002000371

Dearborn Trade books are available at special quantity discounts to use for sales promotions, employee premiums, or educational purposes. Please call our Special Sales Department to order or for more information at 800-245-2665, e-mail trade@dearborn.com, or write to Dearborn Trade Publishing, 30 South Wacker Drive, Suite 2500, Chicago, IL 60606-7481.

C O N T E N T S

INTRODUCTION

For many years we have observed from a distance the ever-present, fast-talking, noisy, Gallery Furniture business owner, affectionately known as "Mattress Mack." Jim McIngvale is a raspy-voiced marketing genius and charismatic leader who has amazed us again and again with his style, energy, passion to help others, and big ideas to entertain and delight customers. Mack is a doer—a ready, fire, aim business icon.

To give readers an idea of the scope of Mack's ability to think big, consider that his retail store, Gallery Furniture, sells more furniture per square foot of retail space than any store *in the world*! Mack has driven his vision to *world class* status. His single-site store in Houston, Texas, sells more than $200 million worth of furniture annually. Gallery stands alone, as the most productive furniture store in the world. That's BIG!

Mack's influence extends far beyond Gallery Furniture. He is one of Houston's most well-known philanthropists and community leaders. You won't read about Mack in the society pages attending this or that ball or gala. He doesn't go in for those things. Mack's philanthropy, like everything else, is done in a straightforward, no-nonsense manner. If a cause catches his attention, he's going to act in a BIG way to make a difference. Whether he's feeding tens of thousands of people at the Convention Center for Thanksgiving, purchasing the Grand Champion Steer at the charity auction of the Houston Livestock Show and Rodeo, or organizing a welcome-home party for Houston's NBA Championship team, Mack ALWAYS THINKS BIG!

Over the years in various business classes we have taught, we have taken informal surveys to determine the person students perceive as the most-recognized business leader in Texas. Since the mid-1980s to the present, Mack is the person most often identified. There is no contest. The second-place person usually receives about 5 percent to 10 percent of the mentions, and Mack gets about 80 percent. Students, like Mack's employees and Gallery Furniture customers, are in awe of him. He is a whirling bundle of energy, a rapid-fire talker who has become a celebrity.

Think of a mix of P.T. Barnum, Walt Disney, Steven Spielberg, and George Steinbrenner all rolled up into a single, dynamic personality. This mixture would be someone resembling Mack. He is a store owner with a flair for entertainment, a reputation for keeping promises, a commitment to doing the right thing and helping others, and insisting with a steel fist on selling high-quality furniture at a fair price. Mack conducts no-nonsense business.

An experience that illustrates Mack's unique and entertaining style involved a sparring match with heavyweight boxer Muhammad Ali. The world champ was conducting an exhibition in Dallas in the late 1970s. At the time Mack was owner of several struggling health clubs. Mack went to the event to see Ali and to promote his health club business. Ali asked if anyone in the audience would like to box a few rounds with him. Mack raised his hand, and Ali told him to come on up into the ring. Mack actually had some amateur boxing training and thought it would be a lot of fun.

When Mack got into the ring with Ali, he immediately knew that if the champ wanted to he could flatten him in seconds. As their sparring began, Mack and Ali moved around the ring feeling each other out. When they got into a clinch, Ali whispered to Mack to knock him down. Ali told him that when Mack threw a punch, Ali would drop like a sack. Then he asked Mack to holler an insulting remark as he stood looking over the knocked-down champ.

Mack thought, if I do what Ali is instructing me to do, these fans are going to riot. But Ali kept urging him to knock him down. Finally, after building up a brief moment of courage, Mack threw a roundhouse punch. Ali pretended like he was hit with a ton of bricks. He dropped to the floor and sprawled on the canvas. Ali, looking up at Mack and grinning, whispered for him to shout an insulting remark. Mack finally looked down and shouted, "I knocked the bum out!" The crowd recoiled, booed, and started to get rowdy. Mack feared that he wasn't going to be able to get out of the building.

Before things got out of hand, Ali jumped to his feet, put his arm around Mack, and roared with laughter. The champ explained to the crowd that everything was fixed. Mack's boxing skills couldn't hurt a fly. The people in the audience roared, and Ali joked and entertained, turning them quickly into a laughing, happy, wildly applauding mob. Mack was in the center of the ring, having the time of his life.

Mack considers Ali the greatest heavyweight boxer in history and a great entertainer. Ali combined his great talent with showmanship to rise above all other boxers. Above all, Ali entertained his customers, the audience. They couldn't get enough of his style, antics, and gimmicks. Mack left this exhibition and his Ali match believing that entertainment had to be a part of any business. Ali was a role model who showed Mack firsthand how to win over an audience by being a showman.

Although Mack couldn't save his troubled health clubs, he has applied the Ali-style, delight-and-entertain approach to his Gallery Furniture customers. The unique and productive retail environment Mack has created provides stunning testimony to the power of a single-minded focus on customer delight. Ali knew his audience loved his audacity and ability to re-create himself again and again. Mack has the same laser focus on his customers, who delight in his ability to make each trip to Gallery Furniture exciting and new.

We have conducted large and small behavioral science studies of executives and managers from around the world. Over 200 companies have permitted us to conduct detailed scientific studies of managerial styles, characteristics, needs and motivations, emotions, and stress levels. Never have we found or been up close to anyone like Mack. He is a force of one, a single, unique character who happens to be one of the most successful businessmen in the world.

We agreed to help Mack write this book to tell his business story and to illustrate his formula and principles for success. We find in the Mack story, style and experience, principles that are applicable in nearly any business. Mack's story is unique, inspirational, and instructional all at the same time. Readers can benefit in many ways, professionally and personally, by examining up close how, why, when, and where Mack thinks and operates.

Some of Mack's behavior is not easy to imitate. At 51 years old, he still works backbreaking 16-hour days too frequently to be admired. He is by his own admission a workaholic. He works hard and with such a passion that it is contagious at Gallery Furniture. Employees and ex-employees respect and love him for being who he is, just Mack. Meet him at Gallery Furniture, and he is the same as when you meet him at a sporting event, charity dinner, or at a speech he is giving in a grade school. Mack's expressed and executed goal in business life is to delight customers. His simple philosophy is:

> The customer is always right. This is the entertainment business. We're here to make sure people have fun. We don't want them walking around like

they're in church. The words, "It's not my job,"
don't exist around here.

Mack expresses this philosophy and how to run a
business in an avalanche of no-nonsense statements.
We met Mack for interviews each Friday morning for
several months before he dashed off to sell furniture, give speeches, arrange sporting and promotional
events, or help others. Some of the meetings were
short, and others were marathons. Interviews were
also conducted with other Gallery employees. We
talked to business leaders who know Mack, students,
noncustomers, customers, and family members. We
also observed Mack on the Gallery Furniture floor selling, ad-libbing an advertisement across the store's
public address system, or physically moving a massive cabinet on the showroom floor. He does everything at Gallery, and he is the image projected to the
public that represents the business. We have used
these observations and direct quotes from Mack to
enhance the lessons so that any manager, marketer, or
entrepreneur can learn from his success.

The core of the book is the 7 principles—found in
Chapter 3 through Chapter 9—that Mack uses as his
approach to marketing and management. He uses
these principles every single day. They are the com-
pass points that guide him to solve problems, make
decisions, and always delight customers. Mack's lessons are applicable to work settings, career manage-

ment, community involvement, and family life. They are specific, practical, and powerful.

Friends, competitors, and critics refer to Mack as a tireless worker, a giving person, a TV personality, and a carnival barker. Mack is many different things to many different people. He is to *everyone* a successful business leader who has blown the doors off traditional measures of success in the furniture industry. Mack uses superior marketing and promotion to continually outsell competitors. He uses simple but effective management to attract, retain, and motivate employees. He is a marketing wizard and an accomplished manager because of his personality, discipline, and powerful work ethic.

Mack is a reader, a listener, and an observer of others. His intense focus and can-do spirit are dynamic. At 51 years old, he has a lot more to do and intends to keep delighting Gallery customers. Along the way Mack will apply his principles. To him these principles are now engrained habits. He still wants to buy and own a professional sports team, drive a racecar, help children become better educated, create more jobs and wealth, and grow Gallery Furniture. Mack is the real deal, the young man who failed miserably, got up, dusted himself off, and tried again until he found his niche. He learned how to market, manage, and delight customers on the job, from mentors, friends, and family members, by reading mountains of books and observing others. He sells furniture from a large, cavernous store on a side road off a busy highway. Mack's story is mostly about his business, his approach to marketing and management, and about people—customers, employees, and the community.

This book provides core principles that can be modified to fit any reader. They are easy to understand and to implement. They are useable in any business or even outside of business. As you capture the essence of Mack's 7 principles, we hope you also have fun and laugh reading how Mack became a successful business owner and leader. He arrived in Houston in 1981 and immediately changed the way furniture is bought, sold, and delivered. As we move through the beginning of the twenty-first century, his principles have plenty of punch and value for anyone who wants to think big and enhance their business and their life.

Tom N. Duening
John M. Ivancevich
January 2002

1

MATTRESS MACK

An Introduction

If you can dream it, you can do it.

WALT DISNEY

It would be great to tell a rags-to-riches tale, but that's not the story of my life. I came from a comfortable middle-class home and background. My early years were filled with leisure and the perks of the upper middle class. I was born in Starkville, Mississippi, but my family moved to Dallas, Texas, when I was three years old.

I went through the Catholic school system with little fanfare—a good student, but not great. I spent most of my autumns on the football field and most of my summers on the golf course. My family had a membership to the local country club, and I would hang out there most summer days.

My mother's name is Angela. She's a strong woman of German descent. She spent her days working as a registered nurse and her evenings running the household, which consisted of three sons, including me, and three daughters. My father, George, was an insurance salesperson and consummate entrepreneur.

My mother's strong work ethic was apparent to me, even as a child. I recall watching her as she worked long and hard to keep the household in order and the family together. There were no explicit lessons about hard work. It was obvious to me that my mother cared deeply about each one of us and that she was going to do whatever needed to be done to keep us together and happy. When you see that kind of effort every day, it can't help but have a lasting influence on you. To this day, I credit my mother for my work ethic.

My father was the primary breadwinner for the family. Dad was often away on business as I was growing up, but his support and love were never in question. I love my Dad, and I admire his practical values and enthusiasm for his work. Dad was a salesperson, no doubt about it. Many salespeople have a problem with the view that people do not look at them favorably. Dad was a salesperson, and he was proud of it. He believed that he was helping his customers solve a problem or satisfy a need. He loved the thrill, the challenge, of selling, and he sold insurance with pride.

Dad taught me to be enthusiastic about work and life. He earned a good living for his family. We weren't rich or privileged, but we didn't suffer hardship. During my childhood years, we were, by most measures, an ordinary middle-class American family. Nothing in my early life or early days in school suggested that I would one day enjoy the extraordinary success that I do today. I credit my Dad's ability to sell with pride, enthusiasm, and sincere concern for clients for having an enormous impact on my personal approach to marketing and selling. I knew early on that I was going to be like him: independent and self-reliant. The 30-year plan of going to work for someone else was never a consideration for me. I'm an entrepreneur. I knew that I was going to start and run my own business. This is my story.

MY FIRST BUSINESS

"What are you going to do next?" my football coach asked me as we sat in the darkened locker room back in 1972. Football season had ended a month ago at North Texas State University in Denton, Texas, and most of the players had cleaned out their lockers and left the campus. Though I was not graduating, as a senior I wouldn't be coming back. Coach Hayden Fry had been through 15 seasons already, but he'd never gotten used to letting his seniors go. He enjoyed coaching, and he enjoyed the camaraderie of the players. I had transferred to the school from the University of Texas and became team captain in my senior year. Coach Fry liked my attitude and heart. Most guys my size—about 5"11' and 170 lbs.—wouldn't think of playing football at the college level. I wasn't big enough to be a linebacker, but that's the position I played. What I lacked in size and speed I made up for in determination and drive. I had become team captain because my teammates respected my determination and grit.

Sitting together in the musty locker room after a workout session in the weight room, I thought about Coach Fry's question. I'm not the type of person who looks or thinks very far into the future. In fact, I had been avoiding thinking about what I was going to do after football. I enjoyed everything about being on the football team—the practices, weight training, and hanging out with teammates. While young and energetic as I was then, I felt a sense of peace and satisfaction from working hard in sports and going home exhausted at night. Now that I was faced with the question of what I was going to do after football, I figured I ought to come up with an answer. I thought quick, another characteristic of mine, and answered, "I'm thinking about opening a health club."

I hadn't really thought about operating a health club before, at least not in any formal planning sense. I hadn't developed a business plan, nor had I done any research to determine whether I could make a living in the health club business. In the spur of the moment, faced with the question about what I would do next, I actually charted the course for the next five years of my life. Oddly, this wasn't at all unusual for me. I have always had the ability to make a decision and, once made, to stick to it. I'd done it before, and it had worked for me. I trust my instincts and have confidence in my ability to live up to my commitments.

I'm spontaneous like that, but I'm not impulsive. When I know something is right to do, I'm going to do it. I knew, after I'd blurted it out, that I was indeed going to open a health club. It fit with everything that I had been doing up to that moment. I enjoyed athletics, I enjoyed working out, and I enjoyed being independent and making my own decisions. Opening my own health club fit with what I liked to do and with who I was. It was not on impulse that I told Coach Fry that I would open a health club. But it wasn't well thought out, either—it was almost as if I had no choice in the matter. Once I stated that I was going to open a health club, I knew that I would do whatever was necessary to make it the best health club in Dallas.

I went home that night and thought more about the health club idea. Now that the decision was out in the open, I found myself getting more and more excited about it. I called my Dad to talk to him about setting up a business.

"Hey Dad," I said, "I've got an idea for a business I'd like to tell you about." "Go ahead," Dad said. "I hope this is better than your last idea", he chided, probably recalling to himself the Japanese cutlery and the herbal diet products that I had previously been excited about. "I want to open a health club," I said. "There's this new type of exercise equipment that people are using called Nautilus. It's really great for people who don't want to work with free weights. It's clean and easy to use. People will be able to come to the club and work out even if they aren't athletic. I know I can make this work."

"Sounds pretty good," Dad responded. "Where do you get the equipment, and how much will it cost?

You'll also need to find a good location and hire good people to run your club when you're not around." I had little patience at that time for my Dad's practical, business side. I really didn't want to think about costs and other business issues right then. I'd figure those out in time.

"I can get the equipment from Nautilus," I stated. "I'm sure they'll help people like me who want to open a club using their stuff. Maybe I'll even sell equipment to people who want to use it in their home." Of course, I didn't know if Nautilus had a program to assist small business owners. I just wanted to get past my father's practical concerns so I could feed my enthusiasm— which at the moment was running very high.

Dad said, "I suppose you should contact Nautilus then. If they're able to provide you with financial assistance, or loan you equipment, I know a real estate agent who can get you a good deal on space for the club."

Now things were moving. I knew that my father would be the practical one. I also knew that he had a network of contacts in Dallas that would help me get the other things I needed—like a location, legal help, and money.

"I can't wait to contact them. I'll call Nautilus first thing in the morning to get more information," I assured my father.

That night I could hardly sleep. Thoughts about how I would run my health club and how I would become successful filled my head. I thought, "I'm going to really love this. I'll be in charge. No one will be able to tell me what to do. I'll have time to work out. I'm sure that I'll be able to open more than one club; there's probably a market for six or more clubs in Dallas, and even more in Fort Worth. I'll get a bunch of people working for me, and then I'll look for other ways to make money. I can even sell Nautilus equipment to people who want it in their homes."

This was the nature of my thoughts as I pondered my future as a health club owner. Within two months, I had found a location and was ready to open the first Nautilus Health Club in Dallas, Texas. The whirlwind that had begun with the simple question from Coach Fry in the empty locker room had swept me up and carried me into the health club business. It was inevitable, really. That's how life was for me. Once I made a commitment, I was going to see it through. The health club express rolled into town and I got on board. Somewhere down the track, however, a loose rail appeared that eventually caused a train wreck, challenging me to deal with failure for the first time in my life.

THE TRAIN WRECK

The health club business seemed easy, at first. Nautilus was helpful in financing the equipment I needed for my club. Real estate was inexpensive. Besides, at that time, people weren't looking for fancy surroundings for a workout. All they wanted was good equipment, track lighting, mirrors on the walls, and clean locker rooms. I figured out how to provide my customers with all the basics without spending too much money.

It wasn't long after I opened my first club that I began thinking about opening another one. The business was attracting customers and growing, and I had hired people to run it when I wasn't around. But I was restless again, and I wanted to expand my health club empire. As usual, I called my Dad to find out what he thought of opening another club.

"Hi Dad, I'm going to open another club. Can I contact your real estate agent? I need to find another good location," I said. Dad replied, "Jim, are you sure you know what you're doing? Opening another club is going to take a lot of time. Are you sure your business is operating smoothly enough for you to take this step? You've only been open for a few months. How about waiting awhile to see how it goes?"

My Dad knew there was nothing he could do to stop me from opening a second club. He knew that I was convinced that opening more clubs was the way to go. He gave me the broker's number and wished me well. As usual, he told me to call him if I needed anything.

Within months of contacting the broker, I had opened a second club and hired a staff. At first, I had concerns about my decision. I found myself spread thin as I chased back and forth between the clubs. There were no mobile phones in 1973, so I became familiar with all the pay phones along the route between the clubs. I frequently interrupted my commute to call and ask people how things were going or to tell them about a new idea.

The second club was turning a profit within months of opening, and my thoughts raced ahead to the idea of opening a third club. I had rapidly become accustomed to the pace and challenge of owning and operating two clubs and was hungry for more. Within a year, I had opened the third club, adapted to the pace of owning and operating three, and begun searching for a location for a fourth.

When the sixth club opened, I found myself on top of the world. I was recognized in many places around town, and local publications began doing stories about my entrepreneurial success. Over a five-year period I had opened six health clubs. I was young, energetic, and on top of the world. Inside, however, I knew that I was no longer in control.

Sometime after opening my third club, I realized I wasn't paying attention to my customers, couldn't watch or examine the business details, and failed to make many scheduled meetings. The old saying, "You can't chase two squirrels with only one rock" fit me to a tee. I'm a hands-on manager, and I want to be involved in all aspects of the business.

I was able to hide my growing uneasiness through the opening of clubs four and five, but club six was the last straw. With six clubs, I could barely spend an hour per day thinking about each one. I grew irritable and suspicious. I lost confidence in my employees, my business, myself. Customers noticed the lack of attention to service in the clubs and began to stay away. It became harder and harder to pay the bills. Finally, when the cash could no longer be shuffled from club to club and from club to creditors at a satisfactory rate, I had to file for bankruptcy protection. I was devastated.

MACK LESSON

On Failure

It's not the falling down that matters, it's the getting up and getting back in the game. You suffer a knockdown, and you get back up—you gotta have that mental toughness. To me it's the same thing in sports or anything else. You've got to have that mental toughness to survive in business and in life because you're going to have problems. You also can't be that concerned about what you haven't had. Look at everything you do have. I see the glass as half full not as half empty. Learn from your failures, but put them behind you and move on.

I underestimated the need for a steady cash flow to maintain all of the health clubs. Once a health club customer pays and begins to use the facility, there is wear and tear that requires more investment in refurbishing and freshening the business establishment. Unfortunately, most health club devotees spend about three or four months visiting and working out. However, most never return after the first few months. This means no steady cash flow from returning customers. Health clubs must always find new customers.

Instead of focusing on delighting customers and my own management style, I was more impressed with the number of stores I owned. The quantitative number and not the profitability of each club was my focal point. The consequence of my inexperience and lack of attention to profitability was bankruptcy. My excitement and enthusiasm raced ahead of sound business analysis and attention to detail.

DARK DAYS IN DALLAS

As the bankruptcy proceedings wore on, I became increasingly frustrated. My biggest problem was the lack of opportunity to work. I was forced to close all of the health clubs, leaving me with nowhere to go. I had a lot of time on my hands but I had no place to work. The lack of work and purpose in life depressed me.

In addition to my growing frustration over the bankruptcy, I was personally running out of money. When things were going well with the health clubs, I wasn't uneasy about going into debt to buy a nice car or to build more clubs. However, now that no money was coming in, I felt the pressure of my creditors. It happened gradually, but it was grinding and relentless. First, I sold my car and began to use public transportation, mostly the bus, to get around town. Next, I broke the lease to my luxury apartment and moved back home with my parents. The final straw, the last move that convinced me that I had lost everything, was when I was served divorce papers.

My first wife and I had not been seeing much of each other for several months. I was too busy trying to save my business to give much time or thought to my marriage. I knew things weren't going well, that my wife was not thrilled with the entrepreneurial lifestyle—constant work, little sleep, no vacations, crushing stress. But I had—and to this day I have—an unyielding sense of hope and optimism that everything is going to work out all right. However, I'm not what you would characterize as a sensitive person. I'm driven and focused on business. I loved my wife, and she probably knew that I loved her. But it wasn't enough. She wanted a husband who had a regular job and who lived a conventional life. Because she couldn't and wouldn't get that from me, she left. Then, she filed for divorce.

I spent days at a time without leaving my parents' house. I felt like a failure. When I looked in the mirror, I thought to myself that I even looked like a failure. A mostly shy and private person already, I was now becoming even more withdrawn. Talking became a burden. My depression began to feed on itself. The more depressed I got, the less functional I became. The less functional I became, the more depressed I got. It became a vicious cycle that anyone who has suffered from depression knows all too well. I had always had something to lift my spirits when things weren't going well—football, weight lifting, business. Now I wasn't sure what to do.

I got a job at a convenience store, but it wasn't much of a job for a former owner of a burgeoning health club empire. One thing that helped to keep me going was a growing relationship with Linda Mc-Cullough. Linda had worked for me at the health clubs. We had started dating after my wife filed for divorce. Linda believed in me. It pained her to see me depressed, and she wasn't about to abandon me. Linda's devotion led her to work side by side with me at the convenience store. In fact, we worked together at a number of stores owned by the same person. It wasn't fun for either of us. Some of the stores were in undesirable parts of town, and Linda's parents were not happy that she was working there late at night. But Linda persevered because she wanted to be there for me. She wanted to help me get through this tough time.

ASSETS AND LIABILITIES

The sun rose on another steamy Texas morning, and I decided it was time to take stock of my situation. I had been working at the convenience store for nearly six months, and I was not getting over my lethargy. I was still living with my parents and had no idea what I was going to do next. Restless, anxious, and a little scared, I decided to make a list of my assets and liabilities. I got out a sheet of paper and a pen and wrote the following:

Mack Assets	Mack Liabilities
Linda	Failed business
Alive	Divorced
Healthy	No college degree
	Living with parents
	Debt
	No car
	No money
	Bankruptcy

My list of liabilities exceeded my list of assets. I probably had more assets than I was able to list at the time, but in my state of mind they seemed limited to the fact that I was alive and healthy, and that I had Linda's support. The liabilities were obvious to me, and they were overwhelming.

Throughout this period, my parents had attempted to accommodate my needs and help me deal with my challenges. They had their own lives to live, but they did what they could to help me cope and adjust. One night, however, my Sally-sad-sack routine got to be too much for my Dad. That night, he came home from the office and found me in the living room sitting quietly alone. He knew I was supposed to be at work, and he knew that I had skipped it. I was lost in thought and didn't acknowledge his presence.

Dad had seen this look about me many times before, but on this night it was more than he could take. I had crossed the line from disappointment over the loss of my business to feeling sorry for myself. My

Dad couldn't tolerate that. He could understand feelings of disappointment. He was disappointed too that the health clubs went broke. He had some of his own money tied up in those clubs—money that he would never see again. But Dad simply could not tolerate the sorry look on my face. Not that night.

"Jim, you look a little down. Anything I can do?" he asked. "No," I mustered. "Well then, maybe there's something *you* can do," he responded, feeling a bit angry at my reluctance to accept his help. "I suggest that you get up off that couch and do *something*. You've been moping around this house for months, and nothing has changed. You aren't even working out anymore. Jim, you've got to do something to get yourself going again."

"I don't really feel like it right now," I said in a monotone voice. "I don't have any interest in anything at the moment."

Dad is an even-tempered man. My family had rarely seen him lose his temper. He prided himself on his self-control and ability to deal with problems and challenges unemotionally. That's why his outburst was such a surprise. It wasn't rage, exactly. It was more like an adrenaline rush. That's what he felt, a superhuman rush to help me, although it sounded harsh at the moment.

"That's it." Dad was on a roll, his voice rising. "I will not allow you to sit here like this and not take control of your life. I've been patient, and I've tried to understand your moods. But I simply will not have you sit here and tell me that you don't have an interest in anything. That I will not tolerate," he declared. Then, the moment of truth arrived. "Jim," he said, "I want you to get out. I can no longer tolerate this state of mind and want you to find another place to live. I'll give you one week. That's it." I sat there silently, staring down at my feet. I didn't say anything—couldn't say anything. I knew I had to find a way to get back my spirit. But how?

THE ROAD BACK

I didn't feel like looking for an apartment right at the moment. In fact, I didn't feel much of anything. My Dad's ultimatum stung a little, but I was down so far that I barely felt this latest blow. The ultimatum had only changed my plans, not my mood.

I decided to visit my sister, Julia, across town for a few days. She would take me in and give me the time I needed to collect myself. When I knocked on her door late that Saturday night, Julia didn't hesitate a moment. She knew I needed a sanctuary, and she was prepared to take me in.

"Can I stay with you a few days?" I drawled. "Dad wants me to move out and I will need a few days to find a place." "Of course," Julia replied without hesitation despite the small house, her husband, and three children. "We'll just move the kids around a little to make room for you. It won't be any trouble at all," she lied. "You sure?" I asked rhetorically. I knew I was welcome, but I also knew Julia's family didn't need a 28-year-old boarder staying with them. "I won't be any trouble. I just need a few days to find a place to live," I repeated.

Julia scrambled inside and raced upstairs to make room for me. The kids were already in bed and Julia's husband, Randy, was in the living room watching *Saturday Night Live.* I ambled into the room and sat on the sofa. I didn't say anything, staring at John Belushi and Dan Aykroyd doing a "Blues Brothers" routine.

"How you doing, Jim?" Randy asked. "Everything all right with you?" "Yeah," I replied casually. "I hope you don't mind if I stay here a few days while I find a new apartment. I'll be gone by Tuesday." "No problem, Jim," Randy said. It really wasn't a problem. Randy and I had a friendly relationship. We weren't friends, exactly. We were brothers-in-law. Still, there was a sense of respect between us that could probably build to friendship if either of us put in the time.

I could hear thumping and crying and Julia shushing the kids upstairs. I felt bad that they had to wake up to make room for me. I vowed privately to myself that I would be out of there as soon as possible.

Julia came down after about ten minutes and told me that my room was ready. I thanked her and shuffled upstairs. Because I didn't have much to think about that night, I fell asleep immediately. After a restless night, I was the first one up on Sunday morning. I quietly crept down the stairs to the kitchen to make a pot of coffee. I gazed out the kitchen window at the early morning mist. "I've got to get back to my normal self," I thought.

My attention was diverted from gazing out the window as I heard the coffee percolating in the pot. I poured myself a cup and sat down in the living room. I was sitting quietly in the easy chair, facing the television set, and sipping my coffee. My thoughts began to wander again. "How did I get here? Why am I sitting in my little sister's living room at this stage of my life? I've got to do something different. I've simply got to get back on my feet."

I'd had these thoughts every day for the past eight months—ever since my business fell apart. They played over and over in my mind like an old cassette tape. My head was tired. I didn't like introspection then, and I don't like it now. I am not good at it. I *had* to change. But how?

Sitting there with the mental tape playing the familiar thoughts over and over, I sought diversion. I reached for the remote control and switched on the television set. It was early Sunday morning, so there weren't many choices about what to watch. I flipped past a few cartoons and landed on a commercial. I decided to wait to see what came on after the commercial. In that instant, the tape began playing in my head again: "What am I doing? How did I get to this? How do I get myself out?" I stared straight ahead as the tape was playing in my mind, and the commercial ended bringing me back to the main program. I was attending to my thoughts and didn't notice at first what program had come on. It was Oral Roberts. Normally, I would flip right on by because I had little interest in television evangelism.

Instead, I sat staring at the television set not paying attention. The tape in my head played: "Why am I here? How did this happen to me? . . ." I shook my head suddenly, realizing that I had drifted from present reality. My attention shifted from my internal thoughts to the television program. I recognized Oral Roberts; I'd flipped past his program on other Sunday mornings. To this day I don't know why, but for a change I decided to listen to what he had to say. I was transfixed as I listened—almost as if Oral Roberts was speaking directly to me sitting quietly in the dark living room at my sister's house.

Are you feeling as if you don't have the power to change? Do you feel as though you've lost control of your life? What should you do about it? Many people feel this way. The problem is, most people think small, and small results are what they get. The solution is to Always Think Big. Think Big and believe that good things will happen. Think Big and strive to achieve greater things each day. You have the choice. Think small and keep on getting small results, or Think Big and strive for goals that stretch you to your limits. What have you got to lose?

LIGHTNING STRIKES

I sat spellbound. I felt as though Oral Roberts was looking through the television set right at me! This was the message that I had been waiting to hear, even though waiting is not my style. I like to take charge, to move ahead. The situation that I was in, waiting for my liabilities to go away, was fueling my depression. "Think Big!" I thought as I sat there. I became increasingly excited and agitated. I was no longer paying attention to what Oral Roberts was saying. He had said enough. Oral Roberts had pressed the stop button on the tape that had been playing in my head. Thoughts about "Why did this happen to me?" were replaced with action-oriented plans about what I was going to do *That Day!*

I knew in a flash that I had to accept my liabilities and use my assets to my advantage. I was alive, I was healthy, and I had Linda's support. It was up to me to use my assets to improve my situation. I knew intuitively that my life would always have its share of liabilities. Everybody has liabilities. I couldn't believe how clear everything was becoming in my mind. "Of course," I thought to myself, "the trick is to continue to use my assets, despite the liabilities. I have to simply keep moving forward. I can't sit and wait for my liabilities to go away."

I couldn't contain myself. My mind was put in gear by the phrase "Always Think Big!" "Of course!" I thought to myself, "That's how it always is. I've been waiting for something good to happen, and I've been making myself miserable. From this moment on I'm not waiting any more. I'm going to take charge of my life again. I'll deal with the court rulings when I have to. I'll even adjust my plans if I have to. But I'm not waiting any more. I'm Thinking Big and going to make things happen again." And I never again waited for something to happen. I now *make* things happen. Alone on a Sunday morning, Oral Roberts had shaken my life and pushed me back into the world.

On Motivational Thinkers

One of the things that I like to do is read books and listen to cassette tapes by self-help and motivational thinkers. I am a fan of positive thinking and credit Norman Vincent Peale, Napoleon Hill, and Tony Robbins with a lot of my energy, enthusiasm, and upbeat attitude.

A good way for anyone to stay positive is to read motivational books or listen to motivational tapes. I don't recommend any in particular. I believe that you should find the messages that work best for you. I recommend that you explore different writers and learn to use their suggestions, lessons, and ideas to improve yourself every day.

I bounced around the house. My mind raced ahead to the things I needed and wanted to do. I needed to find a new job. Working at the convenience store was not helping me at all. I wasn't learning anything new, and I wasn't putting away the kind of money that I was going to need to start my next business. If I quit my job at the convenience store, what would I do? I wasn't sure, exactly. One thing I did know: It was up to me to decide.

The next week was a swirl of activity. I quit my job at the convenience store on Monday morning. My boss wasn't upset about it. In fact, he was glad that I was moving on to something else. On Monday afternoon, I found an apartment and moved in. The security deposit and first month's rent nearly broke me. I wasn't worried though. I liked putting that kind of pressure on myself. "Always Think Big," I thought as I pondered how I would make subsequent rent payments—much less buy food and clothing.

I was back in charge of my life. The new responsibilities that I had thrust myself into were exciting and invigorating. This is what I had been missing! I loved the idea of facing each day with new challenges.

By Tuesday morning, I had decided what I wanted to do next in my vocational life. I had actually been thinking about it for some time. I was a rough and tumble football player, but I have a more creative side that most people didn't know about. From the time I was a child, I had been fascinated with furniture. My mother had a designer's flair, constantly rearranged the furniture in our home, and bought new, unique pieces to give our rooms an elegant finish. I helped her when she rearranged the furniture, and I became adept at helping her pick out pieces that gave each room a special flair. I decided to turn this interest into my next vocation.

EUREKA! THE FURNITURE BUSINESS

"You can have the job if you can work the hours," Ernie said. Ernie was the owner of a furniture store in Dallas. He'd been in the business for 20 years and had seen salespeople come and go. He could usually tell in an instant if a person was going to make it in the furniture sales business. If they had energy and could put in the time and relate well to people, they could make a good living. Most of those who didn't make it washed out because of the amount of time required to make a decent living. To Ernie, I appeared as though I had the energy to be successful; he offered me a job on the spot.

I started working at the furniture store the next day. I was a quick study. I listened to what the other salespeople would say about the furniture pieces and took notes. I wanted to begin meeting customers and to do my own selling as soon as possible. Linda had quit the convenience store when I did, and she had found a job at a local bank. We pooled our resources. Between us, we were barely making enough money to live on. I didn't own a car, so Linda picked me up and took me to the furniture store before she went to her bank job. I worked late each evening. So after her workday ended, Linda would have dinner with her parents and then pick me up and take me home. Occasionally, I would feel guilty about inconveniencing Linda and take the bus to and from work.

That's how things were for a couple of months. I was learning the furniture business, and Linda was socking away whatever money she could from her job at the bank. My spirit had not been tested again since that Sunday morning watching Oral Roberts. I was upbeat, excited, and active. I was myself again, and I wasn't looking back. I learned the furniture business inside and out. I became the top salesperson within five months, working longer and harder than anyone else in the store. I knew that the secret to earning a good living in the furniture business was to please the customer.

After about six months, I began to have thoughts about opening my own furniture store. The health club bankruptcy was behind me, and my divorce had been finalized. I kept my thoughts to myself, for now. I didn't want to scare Linda. Linda, for her part, kept her nose to the grindstone. She and I were becoming increasingly devoted to one another. Although we never discussed it, we began to share the belief that we were going to be together for a long time. Marriage was not discussed; it wasn't my favorite topic at the time. Linda's parents were asking her about it, but she didn't mention that to me.

After a year of selling furniture, I knew it was time to begin exploring my desire to open my own furniture store. However, my loyalty to Ernie prevented me from considering opening a store in Dallas. I didn't want to take any business from him. I knew I could sell furniture in Dallas, and it would be the easy way to go. But I also knew it wouldn't be right. When I thought about where I would go, Houston naturally came to mind.

I broke the news to Linda one evening while we were enjoying a late dinner together at a local fast-food restaurant. "Linda," I began, "I've been thinking about opening my own furniture store." "That's great, Jim," Linda replied between bites of chicken. "What are you going to do for money?" she asked, sounding a bit like my father.

"I have a friend who knows an angel investor who's agreed to invest $100,000, if I can find a good location," I informed her. Linda was not surprised that I could raise that kind of money. I had a lot of friends who were wealthy, although none of them had helped me with my bankruptcy. She was a little bitter about that. But she had no doubt that I knew of people who could invest that kind of money.

"What location do you have in mind?" she asked. I hesitated. I had not thought about how Linda would react to my idea of moving to Houston. Not being a good liar, I blurted, "I want to open a store in Houston. That's where all the growth is." I waited for Linda's reaction. She was expressionless. I studied her for some sign of distress. There was none. Although I had not prepared for this conversation with Linda, she had. She had been preparing for some time.

"I'm not moving to Houston, Jim," Linda said, "unless you marry me first." There it was. Another moment of truth for me. Linda stared at me. My mind raced. "Marriage!" I thought, "Why does it have to be marriage? Why can't we just keep our relationship as it is and move to Houston?" I groped for the right words. What would I say? This was a turning point in our relationship and in my career plans. I had always figured Linda into my plans of opening the store. I needed her with me to make it work—to make my life work.

Then, my practical side took over. I thought to myself, "Where else can I get such a reliable, hardworking, and honest employee?" "OK," I said to Linda. "You've got yourself a deal. Let's get married."

2

GALLERY FURNITURE

The World's Furniture Store

It's amazing what ordinary people can do if they set out without preconceived notions.

CHARLES F. KETTERING

Linda and I headed to Houston in a used, red, Ford truck we bought. The 240-mile trip was filled with debates, plans, and serious talk. I had already purchased a piece of property along I-45 on the north side of Houston. It wasn't much to look at. The property had five abandoned homes on it that were used in a previous life by a homebuilder for display purposes. The only tenants now were cycle gangs, vagrants, and more than a few varmints.

As Linda and I approached Houston, I was excited about meeting with Mr. Dodson, the angel investor my friend sent me to who held the $100,000 we needed to start our furniture business. I practiced different approaches to our meeting over and over again.

27

Mr. Dodson, I really appreciate the confidence you have in me. I will forever be grateful. I want to pay you back within one year.

Mr. Dodson, you won't be sorry. I have everything ready to go and can start selling furniture in ten days.

Mr. Dodson, my analysis shows that Houston is ready for a customer-friendly furniture store. You won't be sorry that you provided us with a start. I will always be thankful.

Linda listened and finally, after hearing too many versions of the introduction and thank you speech, she said, "Mack, be yourself and stop practicing speeches. None of the practice speeches sound like you. They're just too polished."

I wasn't surprised at Linda's honest feedback. I knew she was right. The rehearsed versions of my opening conversation were all off kilter. I'm at my best when I look right into a person's eyes and say what's on my mind at the moment.

Although I knew Linda was right about practicing, I was very nervous. We had about $5,000 and needed the $100,000 to get started. I studied small store furniture sales in cities like Dallas, Houston, Phoenix, and Atlanta by examining available data and literature. My review also included talking to my Dallas mentor, Ernie, because he had over 20 years of retail furniture sales experience. My start-up plan was to purchase enough furniture inventory for at least three months of sales at a cost of about $60,000. We also needed cash to clean up the property and make it presentable for the store's opening. Linda and I wanted to have a fresh and clean property that customers would enjoy.

MR. DODSON'S SURPRISE

My meeting with Mr. Dodson was set for 10:00 AM in an office in the Galleria area of Houston. I arrived at the location around 9:00 AM and drove around for another 25 minutes. I then parked and passed my time by reading both of Houston's newspapers, the *Chronicle* and *Post*. Perhaps reading is too strong a word. I rarely read newspapers cover-to-cover. What I do, even today, is scan the news stories and read and study the help wanted and other advertisements. I am on the lookout for furniture company news, data, prices, and ads. Learning something about my competitors is part of my daily routine. Keeping even the smallest competitor in my sights is a rule of mine. I don't lose sleep over competitors, but I do pay attention to what they are doing. Listening, observing, reading, and digesting what competitors are doing are as routine for me as drinking my morning coffee. I read everything I get my hands on.

I had a plan to become the biggest furniture store in Houston. No one owner had established a #1 position in Houston. It was a wide-open opportunity in a growing and prospering city. Because thousands of people were moving in each week, why not become *the most visited* furniture store location? I had a plan, the vision, and the work ethic. What I didn't have was the money to start.

At about 9:50 AM, I went up to the sixth floor and walked into a bright and beautifully furnished office. I was casually dressed, carrying a black notebook that contained a map of the site for the store. I was nervous. I even stuttered when I introduced myself to the receptionist. After waiting for about 15 minutes, I was shown into Mr. Dodson's office.

Sitting behind a vast, immaculate desk was Mr. Dodson. I introduced myself, "Hi, I'm Jim McIngvale. Everyone calls me Mack. I certainly thank you for taking time out of your schedule." Mr. Dodson hardly looked over when he said, "Mack, I'm glad to finally meet you." Mr. Dodson and I talked for another ten minutes about the weather, the Texas-style rivalry between Houston and Dallas, and my recent marriage to Linda. Everything was low-key until Mr. Dodson looked at me and said, "Mack, I have some bad news for you." I sat up, my eyes focused on Mr. Dodson, and I felt my heart beating twice as fast as normal.

I braced myself for the news. Mr. Dodson said, "After thinking about your location for the furniture store and your inexperience in the business, I have decided not to give you the loan." I was devastated. All of my dreams came crashing in on me.

I finally asked Mr. Dodson, "Why did you change your mind?" Mr. Dodson said, "Mack, furniture is just furniture. Anyone can come to Houston, put up a sign, and compete against you. I don't like your idea to use the money to build inventory, and your location stinks. The site is a run-down, trashy area. Customers will never go there. I've heard a lot about you, but I'm just not impressed with furniture, the North Freeway location, and giving you money to build an inventory."

I learned firsthand from the Dodson experience that when you talk to a potential investor, you must express your vision and plan in crystal-clear terms. I paid too much attention to operational details and not enough on the strategic vision. My plans and vision were muted. My Thinking Big plan to become the #1 furniture store in Houston never saw the light of day in Mr. Dodson's presence.

The discussion continued for another 20 minutes, when his receptionist, announcing another meeting, called Mr. Dodson. I thanked him and left the office. I sat in the truck for about 45 minutes, stunned and wondering how to tell Linda. I could feel my stomach churning just like it did when the health clubs failed. Now what could I do? No loan, a few dollars in the bank, an investor who informs me that the location for my store stinks, and no leads to banks or other investors. Everything looked bleak at that moment. I was a confused mass of mixed emotions—anger, anxiety, frustration, and disappointment. I thought everything was good to go, and suddenly I had a problem. This time, rather than going into depression, I recalled Oral Roberts' advice to Think Big. Instead of feeling down, I felt a surge of energy, excitement, and motivation to solve my sudden problem.

MY NEW PLAN

I drove around for an hour and went over to my brother's home to pick up Linda. When she got into the truck, Linda sensed that something was wrong. She asked, "Mack, how did the meeting go?" "It didn't go," I stated. "Mr. Dodson decided not to give us the loan." "Why?" she asked. "He doesn't like the site for the store," I replied. "He also believes that having the money at the start is not the best way to begin the business. I didn't present my vision and plan clearly. I'll never let this happen again."

I have the resilience to bounce back. Yes, Mr. Dodson had turned me down. Yes, I was devastated. Yes, I was concerned about becoming the #1 furniture store, but I was certain Linda and I could turn this bad news into something positive. I was convinced that becoming #1 in the retail furniture business meant always delighting customers so much that they wanted to return again and again to do business with me. You can delight more customers by understanding a few things about them. Furniture customers are very price and delivery conscious. They want the best prices, and they want their furniture as soon as possible, like today. Furniture customers are very demanding and want to feel good about anything they buy. I studied, analyzed, and observed many furniture customers to reach my conclusions about how to delight them again and again. My customer-delight formula was in place before I opened the Gallery Furniture doors.

My analysis of my strengths, needs, and interests pointed me to the furniture business. Everyone needs a couch, a bed, a table. This is the industry in which I wanted to build my business. I knew what I wanted, and disappointments were not going to stop me. My path, like the paths of most people, was not straight. It was a zigzag, and I accepted that reality.

I broke the silence and said to Linda, "We have $5,000, a site for the business, and a few friends. Here's what we'll do. First, we have to clean up the property. While the property is being cleaned up, I'll continue to work in Dallas and save every penny to purchase furniture. Second, we'll purchase furniture, take out a few newspaper ads, and sell, sell, sell. We'll take our sales receipts and purchase more furniture ads. Sell, buy, sell, buy. We can stock up every Saturday night in Dallas and sell from Sunday to the next Saturday in Houston."

Linda replied, "Mack, that's a plan, but for how long can we physically work at that pace?"

"For as long as we have to," I replied.

The sell, buy, sell, buy cycle can work as long as there are customers, but no customers were going to visit the store given the condition it was in. The first part of the plan involved cleaning up the property, which was a few acres on Interstate 45 that had on it five model homes constructed by a building contractor. It had weeds, snakes, critters, bums, and was, in a word, filthy. Linda and I kept visiting it but usually sat and stared from the truck wondering what to do. Homeless people and gang members would shuffle in and out of the model homes checking Linda and me out from a distance.

Linda and I hired Jose to help Linda with the cleanup when I returned to Dallas. Picking up trash, asking the squatters to leave, and moving dirt with shovels was on each day's to-do list. I worked a few days with Linda and Jose and then returned to Dallas to work for three weeks, to finalize personal matters, to set up a Saturday night furniture purchase plan, and to collect a few of Linda's and my belongings. Linda and Jose worked around the clock, shoveling, cleaning, painting, and finally getting the squatters to leave with the help of the Houston Police Department.

Jose had to use a machete to cut down the weeds surrounding the five model homes. Some of those weeds were over 12 feet tall. It was like cutting through a jungle. We kept in contact and in a few weeks worked out the Saturday furniture pickup schedule. After three weeks of around-the-clock, back-breaking work, the site was finally presentable. The model homes started to take shape and look decent.

THE GRAND OPENING

After all the cleaning, painting, and taking out of newspaper ads, we were ready for our Grand Opening. The plan was to purchase a week's worth of furniture, sell it, and on Saturday evening, hook a trailer onto the red Ford truck and travel to Dallas to load up furniture for the next week's sales. The Houston-Dallas-Houston trip usually took place between 10:00 PM Saturday and 8:00 AM Sunday morning. At 8:00 AM sharp on Sunday, Gallery Furniture would be open for business. The Grand Opening occurred with a handful of customers. There were no crowds beating on the door. There was, however, a complete line of furniture sitting in the freshly painted and cleaned model homes. Gallery was open seven days a week from 8:00 AM until 10:00 PM. Linda and I were on our way.

My plan and dedication to success was burning and passionate. I would sell furniture, move furniture around, help deliver furniture, treat customers like royalty, and think up ways to outsell the competition. I was and still am a fanatic about customer service, customer satisfaction, and especially customer loyalty. I believe that if the customer is delighted every time he or she visits Gallery Furniture, loyalty will follow, and the customer will return. Anyone who came in contact with me learned quickly that the customer is royalty and must be delighted.

Customers Are the Reason for Being in Business

Every interaction with a customer is important. Work hard at pleasing the customer, delighting him or her, making that customer feel important, respected, and valued.

The trickle of customers started to pick up over time, and I learned immediately that delivering furniture when the customer wants it had to become a Gallery promise. I wanted Gallery to be totally committed to same-day delivery. This was an important anchor in my plan and vision of how to succeed in the furniture business. Our competitors doubted that we could stick with the same-day delivery approach. Gallery did, and we continue to prove them wrong. We enjoy being able to occasionally beat the customer to their home with their new furniture. Even today the Gallery delivery truck is waiting for some of our customers as they pull up to their homes. What a treat! Customers with ear-to-ear smiles, surprised to see us with their furniture ready to put it in their homes for them to enjoy. *Today*!

SAME-DAY DELIVERY

I had observed carefully and occasionally first-hand one particular segment of Southwest Airlines' approach to customers and how they repeatedly turned around and cleaned planes to meet schedules. I believed that Southwest's approach to meeting schedules could be applied to the furniture business. Even today, the practice of most furniture stores is to take a customer's order and deliver it in about six, ten, or fifteen weeks. I knew that this gap between purchase and delivery was disappointing and frustrating to customers. Southwest Airlines cut out all the frills and provided passengers with better, faster, and cheaper service. Why not better, faster, and cheaper delivery of furniture?

At the beginning, Gallery was making about ten sales a day. A few of each day's customers would drive out of the parking lot with their furniture. They bought the couch and chair, tied it down in or on top of their vehicle, and off they went. This is still the most efficient way to sell furniture because delivery is an expensive part of the retail furniture business. The customers drive off with their purchase, saving the store money.

I know that selling what you have available and delivering it the same day is what customers want. Customers in conversations tell me over and over that same-day delivery, good prices, good in-store service, and entertainment are what they want. I listen, and every Gallery employee responds.

In the first few years, same-day delivery meant that Linda, I, and the few Gallery employees had to work around the clock. No problem with me. I felt so happy to be running my own business that I was willing to do anything to be my own boss. I was relentless in keeping my promise—buy it today and use it the same day in your apartment or home.

Try It, You'll Like It

Gallery's effort to delight customers creates a buzz. One person tells another, and that person tells another. It's like a forest fire. Word-of-mouth stories about delighting customers are great, plus they're free.

The commitment to same-day delivery was so tiring that Linda and I slept many nights at the store. I also wanted to keep a close eye on the store. To be honest, I was concerned about someone breaking in and stealing the furniture. At the time, our store was in a high-crime-rate location. I decided to stay with the furniture until it was sold and delivered. This often meant sleeping in the store for a few precious hours at night and personally opening the doors at 8:00 AM.

If you asked me about what went on around Houston and the world the first few years after Gallery was open for business, I have to admit I really didn't know. I spent every minute selling, selling, selling. Each day required 100 percent focus on and attention to customers. Our better, faster, cheaper vision didn't leave time to read newspapers, take long breaks, watch television, or go on vacation. I knew this was a tough way to make a living, but I didn't want to fail again.

I had a powerful desire and determination to succeed. What I possessed was deeper than a goal or destination. I had determination to be successful. Every coach has stories about great athletes who didn't make it because they lacked "fire in the belly." They may have had tremendous talent and physical stature, but they didn't have the "fire." Marilyn Monroe wrote in her diary, "I used to think, as I looked out on the Hollywood night, there must be thousands of girls sitting alone like me, dreaming of becoming a movie star. I'm not going to worry about them. I'm dreaming the hardest." This diary passage fits my style. I didn't worry about my competitors. I just worked harder than they did. And I still do work harder 20 year later.

A HERO OF MINE

My determination is a huge part of who I am. I studied firsthand Southwest Airlines' low-price, few-frills, on-schedule, friendly, happy approach to satisfying customers, and also read about and used Sam Walton as a role model. Mr. Walton was a short, no-nonsense, determined fellow who grew up during the Great Depression in small towns in Oklahoma and Missouri. Walton saved $5,000 to open a variety store in Newport, Arkansas. It took him five years to turn a lemon of a store that looked out onto a railroad track into a profitable business. I learned that Walton had to give up the store because the landlord refused to renew the lease. Because of Walton's history, owning my own store and property became a personal goal.

Walton was a workaholic. He would take his family on vacation as long as he could stop and inspect retail stores along the way. I also learn by studying how others operate their business and treat their customers. I didn't even attempt to go on vacation for eight years after Gallery opened. When I started taking vacations, they were business-and-pleasure-blended trips. I would visit furniture stores, look around, watch customers, observe how the store personnel worked, and take notes. I call this practice a "Mack Vacation Safari."

One thing I learned through reading and observation is that there is a degree of fanaticism in some individuals that allows passion to actively destroy them in the long run. Though I am a builder, over the years I have learned to back off when others are smothered by my passion and determination. From time to time I have been too hard on some of Gallery's employees. I still expect everyone to work on holidays, to put in occasional 15-hour work days, to do any job needed to accomplish same-day delivery, and to keep up a fast pace. However, I finally learned that not everyone can work at my pace. So what? As long as they treat the customers right, delight them, and give Gallery their best, I can live with it. It took me years to learn the lesson that everyone is different and to respect these differences.

TAKING YOURSELF LIGHTLY

I have a driven or what psychologists call a "red personality." A few colleagues call me a gold medal "Ready, Fire, Aim" champion. But there is another side to me that needs to be revealed. "The reasons angels can fly," said G.K. Chesterton, ""Is that they have learned to take themselves lightly." I laugh easily at myself.

Having fun, taking myself lightly, playfulness, and humor can contribute to success. A good loud laugh is a regular part of working with and talking to people. For example, I enjoy making people laugh at the way I advertise Gallery Furniture. I know I rapid-fire words, jump around, and appear to have consumed a month's worth of caffeine as I blurt out the "Saves You Money" tag line in television and radio advertisements. It's part of the entertaining, the selling, the making customers feel good.

My 30-second commercials on television and radio appear every 7 minutes every hour of every day. That is about 200 commercials a day. Each TV spot is based on a rapid-fire delivery of words, images of furniture, and me moving around or jumping up and down. My main purpose is to show the Gallery Furniture name brand again and again. I do the commercials in a light, noncerebral manner so that people laugh or smile. I'm not a professional advertiser, but customers and potential customers know who I am, what Gallery Furniture sells, and where we are located.

Helping Customers

A businessperson must always be ready to solve problems. The starting point for solving a customer problem is to show that you are interested by your facial expression and by eye contact. You have to start with a genuine, laser-like interest. Smile, think, smile some more, and help the customer.

MOTIVATIONAL TRIGGERS

Although passion and fun are powerful motivators to me, other factors also motivated me at the beginning of Gallery Furniture that are still powerful today. I couldn't have succeeded without Linda. I don't need a Ph.D. to appreciate Linda's role in my life. I use Linda's conservative business thinking as a counterbalance to my "ready, fire, aim," go-for-it-all approach. Together we formed a team and inspired each other to put in 14-hour to 16-hour days for 8 straight years taking only 3 breaks. What were the 3 breaks? They were the births of our children: James, Laura, and Liz.

Although Linda was more cautious about business transactions, partners, and promotions, she never threw a wet blanket on my passion and enthusiasm. She encouraged me, helped me, listened to me, and laughed with me about life and the business. I surrounded myself with employees who also provided support. If an employee didn't like long hours, selling, treating customers like royalty, and doing what was necessary to deliver furniture the day it was purchased, Gallery was not the place to work.

My support team helped motivate me each long day. In Gallery's early days, our sales approach was to take some of the furniture out of the store and place it in the parking lot in clusters—bedroom suites, dining room sets, couches, chairs. This took a lot of work and coordination. To pick the furniture up, move it outside, sell some of it, and move the rest back in at the end of the day was a wonderful idea that customers liked. On occasion, the skies would open up and pour rain on the furniture. The sight of Gallery employees running around to return the furniture to the store or to attempt to cover it up showed everyone's dedication. I saw this and was energized by my employees. I had surrounded myself with good people, and they motivated me each day.

Absolutely refusing to indulge in self-pity is another motivator for me. After my health clubs failed, I have never again felt victimized. For example, I viewed Mr. Dodson's decision to not provide the $100,000 loan as a problem to be solved. If you are going to have the chance to succeed, there is no time for self-pity. Refrain from self-pity because it depletes your energy, enthusiasm, and commitment. Truck breakdowns on trips to and from Dallas to pick up the week's furniture inventory were no one's fault. Working 14-hour to 16-hour days, sleeping in the store, knowing competitors were laughing at our efforts at the same day delivery were all commonplace. I was not a prisoner or a victim. I have a belief that I have control over my success.

Studies have shown that individuals who have survived physical ordeals—capsized boaters, lost polar explorers, concentration camp victims—all believe that they take their destiny in their own hands. I have similar beliefs. Gallery's future is in my control. I am totally confident in my ability to succeed. The key lesson is that your future, the path you take, and the success you achieve is within your control. Success in business is more about paying attention to detail than it is about luck or fate.

MACK SPEAK

Leading from the Front

My anti-victimization attitude motivates me to want to solve problems. Problems happen to everyone. It's a waste of time to fret about how everything seems to happen to you. If I have trouble with a furniture supplier, I attempt to solve the problem. If a complaining customer wants action, I'm always willing to listen and help. In an argument between salespersons, I will enter the discussion and pitch in to resolve the situation. I believe that when there is trouble, problems, or special situations at Gallery, I am available for action, because this is how I earn my living. You can't operate a business without problems. You can't live an active life without problems.

I try to handle any problems and try to make the best judgment. When I solve a problem, I feel great. The whole process charges me up.

Have Fun

Herb Kelleher, ex-CEO of Southwest Airlines, is a combination of Sam Walton's thriftiness and Robin Williams's wackiness. Kelleher made his employees and customers laugh by not taking himself too seriously. A few examples of his fun:

- *Arm wrestling the president of a North Carolina aviation firm for the right to use the slogan "Just Plane Smart." Kelleher said he lost because of an injured wrist, claiming he suffered the injury earlier when he dove in front of a bus to save a small child.*
- *Attending Southwest Airlines parties dressed as Elvis, a drag queen, and in other bizarre costumes.*
- *Regularly donning a cap and joining the airplane clean-up crews.*

Kelleher was able to instill fun, while delighting his customers, a good example for all Gallery Furniture employees to observe.

My approach of being involved in as many problems as possible may seem tiring. The thing to recognize is that it isn't tiring when you love what you're doing. You can be invigorated by financial, marketing, cost, human-resource, and customer-related problem solving. My philosophy is that you lose your business edge by ducking problems. Keeping a business edge is easier when you jump into tough circumstances at every opportunity you get. Tiger Woods is a good role model because he practices this same solve, solve, solve style in hitting golf ball after golf ball. He practices every day, hits hundreds of balls, putts from varying distances, and works at solving a hitch in his swing, his grip, or his stance.

BUILDING A CUSTOMER BASE

A major dilemma we faced when Gallery Furniture opened for business was twofold: getting customers to visit Gallery and selling furniture. Advertising was a must. One problem I had to immediately face was the cost of advertising. Gallery's financial resources were very limited, but I wanted Gallery to become the most-recognized brand in Houston.

I decided to start with simple classified ads with short descriptions of furniture and prices. In 1981, Houston had two major newspapers, the *Houston Chronicle* and the *Houston Post.* My skimpy 20-word to 30-word ads were placed in both. In addition to these ads, Linda and I prepared flyers with information about Gallery Furniture. Linda would hire a few people, supervise their delivery of the flyers, and cruise to shopping centers, apartment buildings, and neighborhoods putting flyers everywhere. Mailboxes, windshields, light posts, bulletin boards, and any other place a Gallery flyer could be placed or attached was Linda's target of advertising opportunity. Linda supervised the delivery of thousands of flyers to Houston neighborhoods.

The result of the classified ads and the flyers was a steady and growing stream of curious customers. People wanted to see firsthand what all the hoopla was about. At about the same time I observed a wrestling promoter, Paul Bosche, who was constantly on television promoting wrestling matches. Mr. Bosche was an ex-wrestler, a giant of a man, with an expansive style that projected friendliness from his promotional pitch. I watched how Mr. Bosche promoted wrestling by repeating the core message about three times in a 30-second radio or television spot.

I knew that classified ads and flyers would not be enough, so I searched for an opportunity to get on television. Eureka! My first opportunity came when the furniture firm that had used an advertising slot before Mr. Bosche's slot didn't renew its contract. Mr. Bosche had a contract for two 30-second slots. His slot and the furniture company's took up the one minute. I contacted Mr. Bosche and, after a few meetings, my television career was launched. At our first meeting I knew that Paul and I would become close friends. There was a spark of friendship that started with that first handshake, introduction, and eye contact.

The live commercials I prepared and presented created tremendous fear in me. I didn't want to be viewed as a nervous wreck. Paul guided me through my terror by talking to me and coaching me on how to deliver a message to the camera. His help, guidance, and support resulted in my becoming more comfortable in front of the camera promoting Gallery Furniture.

The weekly television promotions resulted in an increased flow of customers. As customers arrived and I greeted them, more and more mentioned seeing me with Paul Bosche. I will never win an Emmy, but I am now completely comfortable in front of a camera. I also know that my fear of being viewed as a nervous wreck was unfounded. I'm an amateur, and I found out that this is what my customers preferred. I am more like a Gallery customer than I am like a polished movie star with an advertising message. My customer base identifies with average, not with superstar. I look, talk, behave, and work hard just as my customers do.

Gallery's customer base since its beginning has been predominantly middle class and every race and nationality. We serve the United Nations of furniture industry customers. We found that no matter how old, what race, what ethnicity, or what gender, if you treat customers like friends, they will return again and again. We also learned that Gallery's middle-class pool of customers prefers the lighter, less-polished advertisement. Some believe that slick, high-powered ads lure customers to a business. My middle-class army of customers has disputed that belief.

I liked and appreciated Muhammad Ali's approach to promoting himself and his fights. "Float like a butterfly and sting like a bee" became his catchy motto. I wanted my own motto. Sometime in 1985 or 1986, I decided to experiment with a new punchline in the Gallery television ads. I placed a number of dollar bills in my back right pocket one evening. As the director counted down, 10, 9, 8, 7 . . . seconds to go in the 30-second spot, I reached back in my pocket and pulled out the dollar bills. I raised them to the ceiling, jumped as high as I could at the time, and shouted, "Gallery Furniture really will save you money!" This tag line is still with me 15 years later. I am often introduced as the "Saves You Money" guy.

WORK REALITIES

As more and more customers visited Gallery Furniture, I knew that the business would be a success as long as I paid attention to and delighted customers. Paying attention means working hard every single day. I look at a few of the defunct dot.com companies and am amused at the typical story. What I hear is that some individual had an idea, spent a lot of money, and as quickly as possible sold the business for millions of dollars. Many dot.com wizards walked away after a quick one-year or two-year run and retired to an exotic lifestyle. I thought I must not be as smart, lucky, or visionary as these whiz kids. Then suddenly, beginning in early 2000, a lot of wizards became ex-wizards with the plunge in the "new economy." To me, the realities of work involve controlling your operating costs, establishing a brand identity, continually delighting customers, and building a loyal customer base.

Writing my own personal job description would be a funny and futile exercise. Since Gallery Furniture opened its doors in 1981, I have been in the customer-delight business, doing everything necessary to earn customer loyalty. A restricted textbook-type job description would drive me crazy. I am the owner, driver, salesperson, complaint handler, financial decision maker, accountant, human resource director, cookie chef, and anything else I need to be in order to delight customers.

I want to be involved in every possible store activity. I can't be everywhere all the time, but I drift and dart around to find out what needs to be done to delight customers. This is how I find out what customers like and dislike, need and want, and how they shop for furniture.

I have found that by working all over the store I not only learn about customers, but I am able to determine what my employees want and need. I believe that my accessibility sends a message to employees that I care about customers. My role is to show Gallery Furniture employees through my actions that customers are kings and queens. I want employees to see me in action and to emulate how I treat customers. If employees are not inclined to be customer-delight focused, their stay at Gallery will be short and not sweet. Other Gallery employees would apply so much social pressure on the nonconformers that staying with the firm would be difficult.

I must recruit and retain employees who understand the furniture business work schedule. Since 1981, the second busiest shopping day of each week at Gallery is Sunday. This means working a full day on Sunday. The same applies to holidays. New Year's eve, Labor Day, and Memorial Day are all big selling times. Putting in time on Sundays and holidays when many people are enjoying picnics, family dinners, and other leisure activities is a part of the Gallery employee's schedule. Anyone not able to conform to that schedule should not apply for a sales position. We are open for business when customers can and want to shop.

3

Establish a Values-Based Culture

I have a simple philosophy. Fill what's empty. Empty what's full. Scratch where it itches.

ALICE ROOSEVELT LONGWORTH

A lot of business owners like to develop a code of ethics for their company. I prefer a simpler approach. We don't have a written ethics code at Gallery. I could probably hire a consultant to help me develop a code of ethics or mission statement, but I don't think those things matter much in day-to-day business. From what I've seen, codes and mission statements are written primarily for people outside the company. That's fine, but I'd rather communicate my values to employees, to customers, and to others through *performance*. We don't need a mission statement to tell customers what Gallery stands for. We *show* them. Every day.

Gallery Furniture doesn't have a written code of ethics, but we do have what I call a "values-based cul-

53

ture." There are so many things in business that you simply can't control. Business cycles, natural disasters, unruly customers, and other events are beyond anyone's ability to control. As a manager you *can* control the values that your employees and your firm live by. These values are apparent in the culture of an organization. Some firms write their values down for others to see. That's all right, but values must be *lived* to be significant. I don't write down Gallery's values or put them in a handbook because I *live* them, and I want my employees to live them too.

To guide employees and build commitment to values, leaders have to practice them every single day. Employees respond to what leaders do, not to what they put in a memo or on the inside cover of an employee handbook. Written statements don't have the impact and effect of direct, everyday performing and *doing.* People respond to actions far more readily than they do to words. For example, when I'm right there in front of people acting on delighting customers, my employees can see and feel my commitment and my passion. It's much harder to convey that emotion in words. One of the things I like to do to show my passion is to broadcast live commercials over the store's public address system. This has tremendous effect on customers and employees alike. I could be like other business owners and leave the work of selling and customer service to others. I don't because I believe that a leader must be *present.* Customers who have seen me on television are often astounded and delighted to see me doing live promotions at the front of the store. This simple practice demonstrates to everyone that I'm committed, involved, and passionate.

A lot of companies give new employees a manual, ask them to read it, and then expect those employees to develop the commitment and passion for the business that leads to outstanding effort and performance. Unfortunately, not many people are willing or able to make that kind of commitment on their own from simply reading a manual. Not many will risk being outstanding, if their leaders aren't showing them that they want and expect them to take risks and to be outstanding. Passive, worried employees are those who are unsure of a company's values. At Gallery, our values-based culture gives employees a sense of confidence and pride. Our culture gives them the confidence to take risks and delight customers.

Some business leaders' egos get so big that it's hard for them to talk to employees. Gallery has over 300 employees, and I know each one of them by name. I meet with the entire company at least four times a year to provide employees with updates on Gallery's performance. We usually meet in the morning prior to opening. The meetings are like revivals. I begin by reminding everyone that Gallery exists for one reason: to delight customers. I like to talk about real life cases and examples of how we please customers. But I don't do all the talking; I ask all the employees to share customer service stories. I usually want at least ten stories before I let everyone leave, but I'll allow more if we're on a roll.

Typically, I'll ask specific employees to stand up and tell the group a customer service story. Many of them are a bit sheepish about talking at first. But I'm not out to embarrass anyone, and I want everyone to have a good time. I'll help out if a person gets stuck. I'll prod them on, asking them to tell us more. Pretty soon, they're standing up there waving and yelling and getting as excited as I do. It's a simple technique, but it really works. It brings all the employees together as a team. People get to know one another, and they get to feel a sense of team accomplishment. When a person finishes his or her story, the group responds with wild applause and the confidence builds. Soon hands shoot into the air as others want to tell their stories and bask in the glow of company-wide approval. Often the most difficult part of these meetings for me is calling them to an end.

GALLERY'S VALUES-BASED CULTURE

Gallery has a values-based culture that consists of five fundamental values. These values were never consciously selected or chosen, but they evolved over time and have been very effective for us. I don't recall how or when they became a part of Gallery's day-to-day operations. These values arose from the successes and failures I've had in business and in life. At any rate, these five values are the ones that Gallery keeps every day, and I think they are timeless values that anyone can put to work in life and in business.

1. Promises Made, Promises Kept
2. Be Honest
3. Thrive on Bad News
4. Be Who You Are
5. Work Hard

PROMISES MADE, PROMISES KEPT

I have never found a value more important than "promises made, promises kept." Throughout my life I have been praised for keeping promises. The accolades I receive for this trait have always amazed me. Why should I be applauded for keeping a promise? Isn't that what a promise is all about? In the last few years, however, I've realized why I'm singled out for this trait: Keeping promises is exceedingly rare.

Because keeping promises in business is so rare, its value is high. You can use basic economics to figure out why that is. The more scarce the product or service the more value people place on it. You've seen this principle in action yourself. When gas is in short supply, the price at the pump goes up—gas becomes more valuable. If you realize that people place value on the personal characteristics of those they do business with, you can take advantage of those that are rare and of high value. I have learned to take advantage of my habit of making and keeping promises and have incorporated that value into my business. People know that when Gallery Furniture makes a commitment to something, it's going to get done.

The number one promise at Gallery is the same-day delivery of furniture or electronics purchased at the store. This promise has been a part of Gallery from the very beginning. The fact that we have been able to *live up to* that promise has astounded and amazed our loyal customers. Gallery chose to build its systems in a way that enabled it to keep that promise. Today, our warehousing and logistics systems are the envy of the furniture industry. Our commitment to the promise of same-day delivery has forced us to be innovative, creative, and systematic. Had we been less than 100 percent committed to our promise-keeping value, we would not have worked so hard and invested so much money to reach this level of success. It was hard work. It required lots of effort to learn how to deliver hundreds of thousands of dollars worth of furniture *every day*. We're still growing and learning because we intend to continue to keep our promise to deliver our customers' furniture the same day they buy it.

The corollary to keeping promises is that you must be careful *not* to make promises that you can't or don't intend to keep. Here's a concrete example. My presence on TV and radio, all the speeches that I give, and the publicity I receive for charitable events that I do get involved in (such as buying the prize steer at the rodeo) have made me a bit of a celebrity. People know me, and they know that I have the ability to be successful with nearly anything I put my time and energy into. Because of that reputation, I get requests to help out in one cause or another literally every single day. However, there is no way that I can help out in each case. To stay true to my "promises made, promises kept" value, I have learned to say *no* to most requests. I have also learned that a firm *no* is the best way to handle requests I can't or don't want to deal with.

When I say "no" to someone, I don't mince words, but I try to be as cordial as I can. I want to make it clear that I won't be spending any time or energy on certain things. Some people find my style to be curt or even harsh, but they always know where I stand. If I'm going to work on a project, I will give it my attention and get it done. If I'm not going to work on a project, I am clear about it to everyone involved. Either way, I leave no doubt about whether I've made a promise or not. I manage expectations by not being imprecise or wishy-washy about my intentions.

MACK LESSON

Managing Expectations

One of the most important principles of good customer relationships is managing expectations. How many times have you as a customer been disappointed because a firm didn't meet your expectations? Many times, the company itself set those expectations—either through a guarantee, a promise made by a salesperson, or through signage in the business. Don't make a promise that you don't intend or can't possibly keep. People expect what you teach them to expect. It's far better to under-promise and over-deliver than it is to over-promise and under-deliver.

We are committed to keeping our promises and to satisfying each customer who comes into Gallery. We're not perfect, but we never stop trying, and we never stop learning. Incidents occur nearly every day that teach me new lessons about a true commitment to keeping promises. The great thing about Gallery people is that we recognize that we're imperfect and, after 20 years in the business, are still willing to learn from our mistakes. I recall one incident where a man bought a big-screen television set from Gallery on a Saturday afternoon. Although Gallery would have delivered the TV that night, the man wanted to take it home right away. So he loaded it in the back of his pick-up truck and drove off. At 9:30 that night, the man called Gallery and stated that his TV had stopped working and that he wanted another one delivered immediately. Gallery promises its customers it will do whatever it takes to make them happy with their new furniture.

My assistant, Myra, took the call. She politely asked the man if he could wait until the morning when a new TV would be delivered. The man was insistent; he wanted to watch TV that night, and he needed a replacement—*now*. Myra is experienced in customer relations and thought she had seen everything, but she really didn't know how to deal with this man. She had never dealt with anyone so insistent on an immediate replacement of a product. Worse, the TV had been out of the store for more than half a day, and there was no telling what might have happened to it. As usual, I was still working that Saturday night, so Myra asked me how she should handle the situation.

Myra said, "Mack, there's a man on the phone who wants us to replace his TV tonight. He picked it up this afternoon, and now it's not working."

"Where does he live?" I asked.

"Crosby," Myra replied. Crosby, Texas is a small town about 35 miles from downtown Houston and about 40 miles from the Gallery warehouse. It would take at least an hour for a driver to get there with a new TV. Factoring in time to load it on the truck and unload it at the customer's house, I figured it wouldn't be in the house and working until after 11:30. What could this man possibly need to watch that night that I should ask a delivery crew to run out to Crosby to deliver a TV—a replacement TV?

"Did he pick it up, or did we deliver it?" I asked.

"He picked it up in his truck and took it home himself," Myra replied.

"Then we don't know how it broke, do we?" I said impatiently. It had been a busy day, and I was tired. I have also seen a lot of scams, and this had all the earmarks of one. "Let me speak with him," I said.

"Hello, this is Mattress Mack, how can I help you today," I said with a hint of impatience in my voice.

"Mack, my TV stopped working, and I want you guys to replace it tonight," the man said.

"Can you wait until morning?" I asked, trying to persuade the man to reconsider.

"No," the man was insistent, "I want it tonight."

I then made what I immediately realized was a mistake, a violation of our unwritten Gallery value of promises made, promises kept. "How do I know what happened to that TV," I said. "We didn't deliver it."

"I'm telling you the TV is defective," the man stated, getting slightly angry. "I want you to live up to your guarantee. Are you going to help me or not? Are you just another phony salesman?"

The last statement stung me. I was anything but a phony. It took only a moment to reply, "We'll get a truck out right away sir," I said. "Sorry for your troubles."

A Gallery truck did go out that night, and a new TV was delivered shortly before midnight. Most people would think that this is a happy ending to a familiar customer service tale. Most people would think that I bent over backwards to please the customer with the broken TV. However, I didn't see this incident as a victory for Gallery's great customer service. Instead, I was upset with myself for questioning the customer's honesty. We would have delivered the TV anyway. Why did I have to question how the TV might have become inoperative? I learned, and I vowed to myself that I wouldn't ask that question again.

Promises made, promises kept is a value that anyone in business should cultivate and uphold. People in business make promises to customers, employees, and others all the time. If your firm does break a promise, you can usually recover by fixing it right away. However, in addition to fixing the broken promise, you should make sure to fix the *system* that created it. One or two broken promises can usually be overcome by apologizing and meeting the customer's needs. Habitual promise-breaking and apologizing, however, is a recipe for losing customer loyalty.

BE HONEST

Truth and honesty in the workplace create a culture of trust. Simple. Yet, how many companies don't get it? They don't understand that simple truth-telling, something we all were taught in childhood, can affect the way people feel and perform. Gallery's values-based culture emphasizes telling the truth. We don't lie to each other, and we don't lie to customers.

MACK CASE

A Culture of Trust

I learned early on that life is much easier with the plainspoken truth as a guiding principle. At Gallery Furniture, this philosophy creates a culture of trust that translates into happy employees and happy customers. Our values-based culture tells employees that we're in the customer business and that we're going to break all the rules to take care of the customer every day. We live the values-based culture that lets the employees know they are important and each customer is important. That's what it's all about.

When people apply for a job at Gallery, we are honest with them about the lifestyle consequences of working here. At Gallery, we work on Sundays and holidays. We tell applicants flat out, "If you can't handle it, don't work here." That level of honesty prevents us from having to deal with thornier personnel issues later. We are also honest about how much money people can expect to make and what we expect from them in their job. We are honest about the long-term earning prospects and the types of benefits we have for families.

The General Rule Is:
People Don't Like Surprises

Honesty is a means of avoiding surprises. Employees want to know what to expect from their jobs, their bosses, and their coworkers. Customers want to know what to expect from their furniture, their delivery, and their warranty. No surprises means being honest about what to expect. How many times have you purchased something only to learn that there are a bunch of hidden costs that you are informed about only after you're standing at the counter with your credit card in your hand? Customers don't like these nasty surprises. They *will* buy from businesses that treat them honestly, and they *will* tell others.

MACK LESSON

Honesty Means NO SURPRISES

You want to be truthful about anything that you may have to prove or deliver on. There is no independent test. Your word is the proof. In business, when you make a statement, you must produce a result to prove it. Don't make any commitments to customers, investors, or employees that you can't prove with results.

Our values-based culture has zero tolerance for dishonesty. From time to time we have had individuals who were less than truthful with customers. If I find out about something like that, I act immediately. Naturally, I do my homework and make sure I collect the facts. If the facts are that the person lied, I fire them. There are no second chances when it comes to being honest with customers. I'm in the furniture business, not in social work. If a person can't live within our values, they can go work elsewhere.

Honesty is also reflected in a company's pricing strategies. We advertise that Gallery has everyday low prices. People come expecting quality and value. We have to make sure our prices and selection match those expectations. With all the advertising we do, people have very clear expectations of what Gallery offers. Any attempt on our part to change our advertised prices or selections would seem dishonest. We advertise to customers the same way we deal with employees: *no surprises.* Our prices, our selection, our financing plans are *exactly* what we say they are—no exceptions.

THRIVE ON BAD NEWS

Successful managers are able to ask hard questions and are prepared for bad news. Bringing bad news to light is something I learned from quality expert, the late W. Edwards Deming. One of Deming's 14 points of quality, discussed in more detail in Chapter 7, is: "Thrive on bad news." After attending many

Deming seminars and hearing him say this over and over, I finally understood what he meant. What Deming was talking about is that, in business, what you don't know can hurt you. Many managers react angrily when someone brings them bad news. What's going to happen if employees begin to fear that angry reaction? You know what's going to happen. The employees will be afraid to report what they know. Worse, they may attempt to hide problems or blame them on someone else.

No business can thrive if the culture is poisoned by finger pointing or fear. At Gallery, we don't like bad news, but we don't get upset or angry about it either. When someone brings bad news to light, we try to look at it as an opportunity. Sometimes it's an opportunity to solve a problem. Sometimes it's an opportunity to please an angry customer. And sometimes it's an opportunity to improve our business processes.

MACK LESSON

No Pain, No Gain

Bad news to a business is like exercise to a person. You've heard the old saying, "No pain, no gain." This means that in order for a person to build a stronger, healthier body they must endure some pain in their exercise routine. Many people avoid exercise and its tremendous benefits because they can't stand the pain. The same is true in business. Many managers avoid bad news and its tremendous potential benefits because they can't stand the pain. Their egos might get bruised, they might fear the reaction of their boss, or they might fear the loss of their jobs. Whatever reason they use to avoid the bad news, the point is, by avoiding it, they lose the chance to strengthen their business.

Not getting angry over bad news may be the most important change I've ever made in my management style. My long-time employees will tell you that I wasn't always accepting of bad news. In fact, I used to have a quick temper and was known for public displays of anger that would embarrass employees, customers, and myself.

My embarrassing displays of anger no longer happen. Now, when someone brings me bad news, I take a few moments to think about it before reacting. People know that I don't like it when things go wrong. But they also know that I'm going to do whatever I can to fix the problem and to make sure it doesn't happen again. Let me give you an example of how I have learned to control my temper and deal with situations by focusing on solving the problem.

One of my top salespersons came to me and revealed that Gallery had mis-priced an entire bedroom suite. Instead of selling the suite set for nearly $6,000, we had sold a large number of the set for just $4,999. This was below cost and resulted in Gallery missing its revenue numbers for the day—a very rare event. In the past, news of this type would have sent me into a rage. I would yell at the person who brought the news. I would yell at the person I believed responsible for the foul up. I would even yell at the people whom I assigned to re-price the furniture. Of course, all the while I was yelling, people around me would be observing my behavior and be making judgments about my character. If I were yelling and raging, most people probably would determine that I'm not worth dealing with when things go wrong. Most would become fearful and decide that it is better to avoid telling me bad news because it would only result in their being embarrassed by my reaction.

Can you see what the results of this fear can be? If someone hadn't pointed out that the bedroom suite was improperly priced, we would have continued to sell it at far less than the correct price. Worse, when we looked at the day's revenue and profit numbers, we would not have been able to determine why they were below normal. It's likely that we would have been alarmed by the numbers, and we would have looked elsewhere for the reason for failing to meet our usual standards. It's also likely that we would have identified the wrong reason for the shortfall. We might have determined that we needed more salespeople on the floor. We might have determined that we needed to increase our incentives or spend more on advertising. We might have determined that it was just a bad day, based on the weather or some other uncontrollable factor. Whatever reason we would have found, we probably would have missed the obvious and easy-to-fix reason: Someone had made a very human error and mis-priced a suite of furniture.

Dr. Deming taught thousands of managers to thrive on bad news. It took me many trips to his seminars to finally understand what he was talking about. Business is a system. To be successful that system needs to be tuned and adjusted from time to time. An automobile system has warning lights and buzzers to let you know when it needs to be adjusted. Managers of businesses don't have warning lights, but they do have something potentially more effective—their employees. A firm's employees are usually the first to know when a system is out of whack. They should be trained and empowered to fix or adjust the system when they can. They should also be trained to bring the problems to light. As I did, managers should learn to control their reaction to bad news and recognize bad news as an opportunity to make the firm stronger.

BE WHO YOU ARE

Being who you are means allowing yourself to be genuine—no pretenses, no false pride. Most people who know me would probably tell you that I tend to wear my thoughts and emotions on my sleeve. Because of that, it's easy to be truthful with others, and that makes it easy for them to be truthful with me.

I've met many business leaders who are so full of themselves that other people can't stand to be around them. These leaders might possess great talent. They might be beautiful or handsome. They might be extremely intelligent. I say, "So what?" At the end of the day, all that matters is results. You can be the smartest person on earth, but if you don't produce results, your intelligence isn't worth anything. This simple truth applies to *everyone*. Every one of us must produce results to live and thrive. This requirement puts us all in the same boat. No one is immune—not the beautiful, not the rich, not the smart. I don't have time for people who can't help produce results because they think they are somehow better than others. At Gallery, I'll do anything to keep the furniture moving out the door. If that means sweeping up at 11:00 on Sunday night so we can be ready to open on Monday morning, I'll have a broom in my hand like anyone else. Why should I be too good to push a broom?

Being transparent around your employees is the first step in letting them know you care—about the business and about them. People respect those whom they can identify with—people who are just like them. You can build on that respect in numerous ways. One example of a simple gesture that paid off big with my employees occurred in March 2001. I was sponsoring Wrestlemania XVII. The World Wrestling Federation (WWF) and its consummate promoter, Vince McMahon, has been attracting huge television and live audiences. The WWF has a rapidly growing fan base in the hottest market segment—17-year-olds to 34-year-olds of all races and both genders. Because this demographic segment overlaps with the people who buy furniture at Gallery every single day, I decided to get involved and sponsor the wrestling event.

Wrestlemania XVII was held at the Houston Astrodome, the first domed stadium. Built in 1964, it was billed at the time as the eighth wonder of the world. The Astrodome has been the scene of a number of major events over the years, including one of the all-time-greatest and most-watched college basketball games, the one between UCLA and the University of Houston in 1968. The Astrodome is home to the annual Houston Livestock Show and Rodeo, and it has hosted the Houston Astros baseball team and the Houston Oilers football team. The Houston Wrestlemania XVII event attracted the largest crowd ever to attend a live event in the history of the Astrodome, with millions of additional viewers on pay-per-view TV.

As sponsor, I had a number of ringside tickets and was expected to be there as a VIP. I knew that many of my Gallery employees were big wrestling fans and wanted badly to be able to attend the event themselves. However, Wrestlemania XVII was held on a Sunday night—a work night at Gallery—and many of the employees couldn't afford to take time off. With help from my assistant, I worked it out. We gave more than 20 Gallery employees the ringside tickets. To compensate for their absence at work, my assistant and I stayed all night at Gallery to help get their jobs done.

It was no big deal for me, really. I missed Wrestlemania—the glamour, excitement, and large crowds—to work in the Gallery warehouse, loading trucks for same-day delivery. My people appreciated it, and they'll be in here working all the harder to see that our customers are delighted. Simple gestures like that let people know that you value them as much as you value your business. After all, it's your people who are out there meeting customers—they meet them in the store, on the street, and at Wrestlemania. Isn't it better that they say good things about their employer? I have always felt very good about feedback I get from parents, wives, or others who know a Gallery employee who enjoys our work environment.

How many CEOs would miss the opportunity to bask in the limelight of the event they sponsored? How many would give their most expensive tickets to their employees and then work their shifts—in the warehouse? No big deal for me. I knew those employees wanted to go. By my just being "Mack" around my employees, they can be themselves too. I want everyone to feel that they are appreciated for what they can contribute to the Gallery cause. If people feel that they have to be more than they are, you end up with the famous Peter Principle: They rise to their level of incompetence. In most companies, people continue to rise up the corporate ladder until they hit their own personal glass ceiling. At Gallery, we want people to contribute according to what they do best: The profit-based bonuses that we pay are just as large for the managers as for the warehouse workers. Everyone benefits, if people leverage their strengths and be who they are.

WORK HARD

It may sound weird, but hard work is easy for me. It's easy because I just don't know any other way. I've been working so hard for so long that I'm unhappy when I'm not working. It's important to recognize, however, that hard work doesn't mean I'm going to make a lot of money. My motivation for working hard is different. I'm honestly driven by the desire to please customers. I take the most delight from the expressions of satisfaction that I hear from customers each and every day.

A lot of people go into the furniture business to emulate Gallery, but they forget about the 100-hour workweeks. While my competitors are thinking of making money for vacations, golf, and other things, I'm thinking about customers. I get up in the morning thinking about customers, and I go to bed at night thinking about customers. My whole life revolves around my store, my employees, and my customers.

MACK SPEAK

The Essence of Business

You buy it, you sell it, you go get some more.

I had a lot of dark moments in my business career. The first ten years at Gallery were day-to-day survival. I can't tell you how many times we had to fight to make that last sale at 10:00 at night to be able to make payroll the next day. It's hard to do, but I kept the faith the whole time. All the positive sayings I learned when I was a kid only served to make me stronger. I just kept listening to those positive voices in my head, and that helped me through it. It's tough out there. There are a lot of competitors in the furniture business. To deal with it, you have to have mental toughness.

To succeed in business, you have to work hard and stay focused on the task. I'm like a plough horse. I go down to one end, turn around, and go back to the other end. I don't let myself get distracted from executing in the business. You know the age-old story about the tortoise and the hare? I'm like the tortoise. I just keep on going. All these rabbits out there seem to be doing better than me, but they go golfing, or they go on a long vacation, and they take their eye off the ball. I just keep on going. One day, they all look up, and there I go walking across the finish line before anyone else. My advantage is that I honestly believe that no one is able to work harder than I can. That's a nice advantage to have because I'm responsible for it, and I'm not about to let my guard down.

The Gallery values-based culture includes hard work because that's what it takes to be successful in the furniture business. When we hire new employees, one of the things we look for is the ability to work hard. We often get resumes from MBAs who want to join the "executive team." Funny thing, we don't have an executive team at Gallery, and we don't have many

MBAs. Many Gallery employees have high school diplomas or GEDs. They work hard and make a good living. Gallery recognizes and rewards this hard work with a profit-sharing plan that is among the most generous in the industry.

Our hard-work value rounds out the Gallery values. We create opportunities for each employee to work hard in a number of ways. Each employee is encouraged to work as often and as long as they can. Each employee is also encouraged to be an ambassador for Gallery while away from the office. You'll never see me without a Gallery shirt, hat, or other indicator of my association with the store. Many of Gallery's employees also proudly display the Gallery brand on their clothing, cars, and in their homes. They're constantly working with me to build the Gallery brand and live the Gallery values.

WORK AND SPIRIT

I'm convinced that a values-based culture translates into happy employees. If Gallery employees believe they are being treated ethically, they really don't have to worry about job security and other distracting issues. If they believe that they can count on Gallery—and me—to treat them fairly, they don't have to worry about *keeping* their jobs and can concentrate on *doing* their jobs.

Everyone needs to create and follow his or her own values. My personal values are derived from my Catholic upbringing and background. I don't usually talk much about my faith, but it is a part of my life and has become increasingly important to me over the years. On a trip to Rome in 1992, I was struck by the beauty and grandeur of the Vatican. While I was there, I felt something inside that I call a religious experience. It wasn't mystical or overwhelming, but it was profound for me and has had a lasting effect.

After the Rome trip, I decided that I wanted to get back into a routine of attending church on Sunday mornings. Luckily, one of my employees who has the ability to open the store herself attends church regularly on Saturdays. She agreed to open the store on Sunday mornings so I can attend church.

Attending church service has become a sanctuary for me. I enjoy the peace, the ritual, and the fellowship. I still don't talk much about my faith or ask others about theirs. My faith is a private matter, and I mention it here only to get across that I have learned to recognize the value of having a peaceful place for reflection and renewal. Every entrepreneur or businessperson should find his or her own personal sanctuary. Whether it is a church, a cottage by the lake, or a quiet corner of the house, everyone who works hard and wants to be successful needs a place where the demands of business are released—if only temporarily.

Despite my recommendation that all business people need a sanctuary, there should be no mistake on this point: I'm a salesperson. I sell furniture and try to make a profit. To my way of thinking, there's nothing incompatible about having faith in God and being an honest, hard-working businessperson. Some people believe that capitalism and spirituality don't mix. I disagree. I think God wants everyone to make full use of his or her capacities as a human being. My goal—my mission in life—is to sell furniture better, faster, and cheaper than anyone else. I really believe that I am being true to my faith and myself by doing what I do. That gives me peace of mind and a sense of confidence, allowing me to focus entirely on my business and to try to delight each and every customer who enters Gallery.

FINAL THOUGHTS

Applying the five values—promises made, promises kept; be honest; thrive on bad news; be who you are; and work hard—in business and in life doesn't guarantee success. Nothing can guarantee that. Because many things are beyond the control of the businessperson, success requires a large amount of luck as well as skill. I do know one thing, however, and that is *discipline* and *commitment* to values are *necessary* for success. Living and working according to the values of keeping promises, living honestly, learning, being true to oneself, and working hard set the stage. If success is to happen, it is far more likely to happen to those who have invited it into their lives through discipline. Being disciplined to live according to a select few values is not a once-in-a-while thing. It's an everyday thing. If you want to be successful, you *must* be disciplined to live your values every single day.

Go Forward!

It took me 48 years to determine who I am. I did one of those personality tests where you answer all these weird questions to determine who you are. Well, I found out that I have what's called a "red personality." I've got to go forward. That's me. I'm driven. My personality is 100 percent go. There ain't no back up in me. When the computer goes down or the business stops, that's when I get really frustrated and feel helpless. But when we're moving forward, we're taking care of those customers, we're shipping the furniture and making people happy, that's what energizes me the most.

4

FAST—Focus, Action, Search, and Tenacity

When an archer misses the mark, he turns and looks for the fault within himself. Failure to hit the bull's-eye is never the fault of the target. To improve your aim, improve yourself.

GILBERT ARLAND

Like most people, I want to be successful. My first noticeable desire to be successful started with sports. I dreamed of being the best football player around. It didn't deter me that my lack of size, speed, and strength would be obstacles. I just was full of desire to someday play for the Dallas Cowboys. I let this dream open the window on every possibility to succeed. Along with my personal dreams, all around me I received encouragement from my family, parents, and coaches.

One day, after years of thinking about my dream and evaluating my progress, I realized that playing on Sundays with the Dallas Cowboys was not going to be

79

possible. What a blow! Reality finally smacked me in the face and took hold of me. My dream had motivated me to work at becoming a better football player in high school and college. I did become better, but I never reached the skill and talent level needed to find success in the National Football League (NFL).

But I did learn from my early football playing days that I needed dreams, goals, and focus. This combination helped me learn how to concentrate on what I wanted to accomplish later. My Dallas Cowboy player dream was replaced by my business dreams. I've been living with this entrepreneurial dream now for over 30 years.

Today, I still dream, but I use goals and a laser-like focus more than dreams to guide me each day. I have a formula and use the acronym FAST as a reminder. My formula is straightforward: F is for focusing on customer delight above all else, A is for taking action to make my focus come true, S is to search for the right adjustment when results don't match goals, and T is for tenacity, never quitting until I reach the goal. This is my goal focus device: FAST. It works for me and has become my tool to staying on course and succeeding. It's up to me to succeed at Gallery Furniture. If Gallery is going to be successful, I need to focus on dreaming, goals, action, search for alternatives, and tenacity. By using this approach the results take care of themselves. There's nothing mystical about my FAST formula. These four focus steps have worked for me when things were going great but also when the bottom was falling out.

Ford Delights Customers: In His Mind

Henry Ford used mental pictures to get his company started. He pictured in his mind the type of automobile he wanted to build at a price the public could afford. He created a mental movie of his dream Ford car long before engineers designed it and prepared a model. Ford also pictured masses of people buying, driving, and smiling in the car. He saw delighted customers in his mind and had no fear of failing.

F = FOCUS

I have learned to focus on such concepts as "same-day delivery," "promises made, promises kept," "being friendly," "providing top value to customers," "always surprising pleasantly," "the customer is right," and "listen to what customers, employees, or suppliers are saying." I focus my energy, my time, my thinking on a few top-priority, must-do goals. When a customer is complaining about the couch they purchased, I focus on the person, the words, the complaint. A car can drive through the front door and I won't notice it because I am so focused. Focusing is hard with everything swirling around—the noises and the interruptions. I have learned to focus with a special kind of laser-like concentration that is difficult to break.

Some business owners or managers focus on what the competition is up to and then react. A certain amount of competition will always be there tugging on customers. Instead of focusing on competitors, I recommend that most of your attention, energy, and effort should be on customers. By concentrating on your customers' needs, wants, loyalties, problems, complaints, and wishes, you can take appropriate action, adjust, and persist so that they are delighted. Focusing on customers is my top priority and my key to Gallery's success.

Focus Is an Everyday Job

One of the problems in my health club business was not paying attention to my customers. I learned through experience that the first day a health club opens, everything is working, the facility is immaculate, and the place smells new. From that first day on there is wear and tear. Customers prefer new, fresh, and efficient to old, stale, and broken facilities. Instead of finding ways to delight the health club customers, I drifted. My concern shifted to building a network of health clubs. I started to focus on the competition and the ego need to own more clubs. My customer-delight focus was overwhelmed by a "Mack needs more clubs to outdo his competitors," which was definitely not the right or smart focus.

At Gallery, customers want new, fresh displays and new color schemes and themes. They expect to be delighted, to be entertained, and to receive the best deal. I know this because I listen to them. I focus on what they tell me over and over. Because customers want new and different furniture configurations, we give them what they want: Gallery is constantly changing the layout, furniture arrangements, and color schemes in the store. We make adjustments to fit the eyes and tastes of customers.

To keep my focus, I talk to myself. I repeat the words "customers," "success," "problem-solving" every day. This has become a habit. It is my daily affirmation, my to-do approach. It is also my "never forget" reminder. It is my habit to say these words out loud while driving to and from work. Even when I am dog-tired coming home, late at night, I sometimes say the words out loud.

My focus habit and affirmations influence my daily calendar. Every day I am in contact with customers because I need to solve problems. Skipping customer contact is not acceptable. Some customer situations are unique but are very important for learning. For example, recently I had a customer referred to me who had purchased a couch four months ago. He wanted a full refund on the couch because it didn't fit his needs perfectly. "Wow!" I said. "Four months is a long time. I can't resell this furniture." I knew that this would be a loss to Gallery, but I thought about tomorrow. This customer might remember how Gallery treated his return request. I agreed to swap the couch out. My business sense said, "No way," while my customer focus said, "Okay, I'll do it." I am not recommending swap-outs after four months. I solved the problem by listening to the customer, focusing on his distress, and deciding to swap out this couch. I didn't provide the automatic "no." Yes, I probably lost money on that deal, but my focus, or concentration, pushed me to take a chance. I'm also not recommending always making this kind of concession to a customer. What I want to illustrate is that the customer's request and preference are important to my success and must be evaluated on a case-by-case basis.

One way to find out what to focus on is to ask yourself and then listen to the answers that come up. Some of the answers are silly, offbeat. The major focus point for me is customer delight. This is my focus bull's-eye. I keep my mind working on this target every day. I don't count success in dollars. Instead, success is doing what I love to do: Delighting customers by selling them furniture and promoting Gallery. I don't consider customer delight a one-time effort. It is an ongoing struggle. Remember though, as you delight customers, their expectations increase. You have to continue elevating the surprises so that customers are delighted all over again.

MACK SPEAK

Making a Person a Customer

Getting people into the store is not even a halfway victory. You have to focus on them and earn their confidence, which turns them into a loyal customer. Don't celebrate just the numbers who come through the front door. Once they are in the store, you have to creatively satisfy their needs. Making customers love doing business with you is a powerful reason why they will keep coming back into the store.

A = ACTION

A focus gives you a target. Taking action and moving forward gives life to focus. When I act, I set things in motion. By setting things in motion, I move from being a dreamer to being a doer. When Linda and I first set our eyes on the weed-infested store site, our dreams of operating a successful business at the location became hazy and confused. We dreamed for so long without doing or acting that for the moment we became discouraged. We forced ourselves into action with a clean-up, fix-up plan. We became doers. We made a commitment to clean the site up and open the store a few weeks later. Our plan worked, and it taught me that dreaming is not enough.

Leaders must act to overcome the immobility of simply dreaming. Instead of focusing on a sales growth goal in my furniture business, I learned to take small action steps. For example, I worked hard at listening to customers. It is easy to avoid a customer with a complaint. However, a customer who believes he or she is not respected because of inattention will go elsewhere to buy furniture. If you lose a customer's annual sales for, say, ten years, you lose a lot of revenue. Lost customers are hard to replace. My small action steps—listening attentively, being friendly, smiling, providing popcorn for customers' children—all add up. Instead of focusing on a grandiose growth goal, I encourage you to learn how to focus by tackling smaller bite-size goals. Smaller action and results are better than waiting around for the "big bang" goals to be achieved.

I've learned that action, initiative, and self-motivation will put you into the middle of the business give-and-take. From the time I set foot on the Gallery Furniture floor each day, I am in action physically, mentally, and emotionally. Tom Peters, the management consultant, coined the phrase "management by walking around" (MBWA). He coined the phrase, and I live it every single day.

Find a Favorite Affirmation

Here are a few action phrases I enjoy.

- *If it is to be, it is up to me.*
- *Excellence can be attained if you expect more than others think is possible.*
- *A leader is a person who will get you to a place you wouldn't get to by yourself.*

Another part of my action-now approach is to be positive. You can't just turn on a switch labeled "positive thinking." You can't attend Harvard and receive a "positive thinking" degree. I find that whatever I do in business, in my family, or in the community, positive thinking is a part of the action. When I'm confronted with a customer problem, a furniture manufacturer delay, a blinding rainstorm on a usually busy, big sale day, I think positively. You might say this is impossible. No, it isn't if you work at it. I made a conscious decision after my business failure in Dallas to change how I think. I decided to become a great furniture business owner and leader.

When I made a decision to stop feeling sorry for myself, I saw my opportunity to be successful in business become visible. I had to work hard to change how I thought so that my action, energy, effort, and whole being reflected the change. A positive attitude is built around three concepts: energy, not whining, and being committed.

Code Words

In order to take action, to overcome the tendency to just dream, you must be energized. When your energy is low, your actions usually sputter. Low energy results from having worked too hard or from doing something you don't enjoy. If you are not challenged by the actions you take, you feel flat. This means that you have to learn how to pump yourself up. Self-talk is one pumping technique. Telling yourself what you have to do and how to do it is a starting point.

I was told again and again by so-called furniture industry experts, competitors, and manufacturers that my dream of same-day delivery was impossible to turn into reality. One competitor in particular mocked my dream. I used the doubter's words to pump myself up and to seek out ways to accomplish same-day delivery. Four years after he laughed at me, I bought out his furniture store when he went bankrupt. I was not happy about his failure. He was a man attempting to succeed. I respect and honor him for his effort. However, I was very happy to have overcome his negative thoughts and his mocking of my dream.

The image I still use to pump myself up is being viewed as the originator of same-day delivery. In athletics, a phrase, "parking the fatigue," is used to express the idea of putting a tired feeling on the shelf. To accomplish same-day delivery requires a lot of "parking the fatigue." Drivers, warehouse handlers, sales personnel, clerks, and all employees involved get tired because of Gallery Furniture's pace. Most employees are able to be tired later or after the furniture is delivered, and the customer is delighted. I personally energize myself by using code words like "do it now," "out of my way," "Mack explosiveness," and "will do right now." These words remind me of the desired results. I use these phrase cues when I need a positive boost. You can prepare your own code-word boosters. Take a few minutes and prepare a few of these code words for yourself.

It's common to feel less than positive if you think you have no chance of succeeding in the action plan you are using. I have to fight against feeling lethargic and low in energy. I use music at Gallery to pump up energy levels of the employees and customers. Because some of my personal music choices are laughed at, we try to play all kinds. I also engage in my own Mack aerobics program: walking fast around the store to stay energized. I also move furniture, call meetings, and bark out advertisements in the store microphone, all of which keeps me moving. Being energized allows me to walk, talk, and act fast for 14 hours to 16 hours each day. My pace keeps me breathing deeply, moving vigorously, and sleeping soundly when I arrive at home after a tiring day.

I have found that by being energized I influence Gallery employees and customers. By being energized, focused, and passionate, other employees feel good and feel a sense of excitement. The people I interact with join in and build my energy and excitement. I laugh, sing, wheel around the store, celebrate sales, talk into the store's microphone, and pump up the energy for myself and others. I'm not afraid to show emotion or that I am energized.

Not Whining

I refuse to come up with excuses. If one of my ideas doesn't pan out for selling furniture, it is my responsibility. I had a salesperson who, during a downturn in the economy in Houston, told me that his sales would be down until everything improved. "People are not buying any furniture. Mack, we are going to be in for a dry spell." His energy level was low, and he lacked confidence in his ability to make sales. Another salesperson considered Houston's economic downturn as an opportunity to sell more. "Mack, this is the time to cut deals. People are watching their money more closely, but they still need furniture. I have got to be a better salesperson, but this is a great time to sell."

The two salespeople were faced with the same economic conditions but viewed the situation differently. Eventually, the first salesperson quit the business. The second salesperson hung in there and is still one of Gallery's most productive, high-energy employees. She made something good happen for customers. She focused, listened, innovated, and kept a high energy level.

Blaming others is not a path to success. You will find that when someone blames others, it becomes an excuse, a reason to not work hard, to plan, and to be energized. Don't waste energy or time blaming others. It creates a barrier for action. Look at yourself, your reasoning, and your approach if a failure occurs. In the furniture business, rejection occurs every day. You think a customer is going to buy and suddenly decides not to. I quickly revisit what happened. I try to learn at least one thing from not succeeding. I then just move forward to the next situation, the next customer, the next challenge. Whining about a failure, a mistake, a setback is just not productive.

Be Totally Committed

Being totally committed helps me maintain a positive focus and attitude. I have found that many people put a qualifier into their commitment-thinking. "I'll learn how to operate a computer program 'as long as it's not too difficult.'" "I'll really sell a lot, 'when the economy improves.'" When I make a commitment, nothing will stop me except a health problem or a force beyond my control. I may have to make adjustments, but nothing will stop me. Uncertainty, overcoming obstacles, and failing are all a part of intensifying my commitment.

I give over 300 speeches a year to groups such as school boards, Rotary Clubs, Chambers of Commerce, religious groups, veterans clubs, and college classes. I commit to each of these groups. Schedule, travel, and other unexpected problems, including family crises, occasionally pop up when a speech is set. Yet, I rarely miss making a speech because I made a firm commitment to talk.

I have meetings with employees scheduled to discuss ways to delight customers, new sales promotions, work schedules, bonus-sharing plans, and many other topics. Each meeting is a commitment to interact with the Gallery family. An employee wants to ask my advice or inform me of something, such as a personal problem with one of her children. Because I made a commitment, I am there on time with all of my concentration and focus on the employee's needs and wants.

A leader must be committed to his or her business, employees, and customers. This builds a deep bond of trust. The trust bridge goes both ways. The people I make commitments with trust me, and I build my trust and confidence in them.

Committing to my business dream is an ongoing process. I commit to Gallery Furniture every single day. The test of my Gallery commitment is my action. After 20 years, I still demonstrate by my energy and work ethic that I care for customers, employees, and the community. I am serious, but I have fun and laugh at myself and others.

S = SEARCH FOR ADJUSTMENTS

Finding the best possible adjustments is a necessary part of being in the furniture business. I change prices, rearrange furniture, redo advertisements, and constantly search for ways to delight customers. It makes no sense to keep ramming your head into an immovable wall. Find a new way. Go around the blockage, the barrier. I use my own go-around, go-under, or go-over approach when something doesn't work. I keep searching for ways to sell more furniture and to delight customers. I'm a man of a million options because I search for adjustments.

For some reason, people sometimes give up trying in carrying out their career, life, or personal plan. I find no solid or acceptable reason to give up when goals are being missed or undershot. Explore new avenues. It's like Tiger Woods who constantly makes adjustments in his golf game. He experiments, tries new things, and is constantly staying flexible. This is the style of the world's greatest golfer. He is great, but he continues to adjust. He creates options when it seems impossible. I also am a creator of options.

One of the biggest adjustments made at Gallery Furniture was to take all sales personnel off commission. For years, Gallery sales personnel were paid very well if they sold furniture. The commissions were exceptional, but the teamwork and morale consequences were devastating. Competition was so fierce that cooperation and teamwork among sales personnel was practically nonexistent.

I personally was appalled at how some of my sales personnel treated each other. This poor treatment splashed over onto customers. For example, when a Spanish-only speaking customer entered the store and an English-only speaking salesperson met the customer, there were stares, hand gestures, and little productive communication. The salesperson failed to help the customer satisfy his or her needs. The competition for the sales commission was so intense that the delighting of customers became a secondary consideration. You can't succeed in a business where customers are not being served and delighted.

I studied the sales personnel pay system, read about compensation and motivation, asked some experts their opinions, and decided that a major adjustment was necessary. The commission system was put out to pasture because it didn't help Gallery delight customers. It also was put away because it created dysfunctional competition and little cooperation. The Gallery sales force consisted of teams of one person each. Yes, each salesperson was his or her own island, working to generate healthy commission-based pay. The straight commission gave way to the salaried furniture salesperson. The result of this adjustment has been increased cooperation and still some competition to sell, delight, and service customers. To be the best on a team of great sales personnel is now what Gallery strives to accomplish. New sales personnel and the experienced salespeople now cooperate more than I thought was possible.

Adjustments have been made in many areas at Gallery because they were necessary. I observed that most customers had young children tagging along as they shopped. The kids looked bored, some cried, and some actually tugged at Mom or Dad to get out of the store. Linda had for over three years told me to build something for children to take the load off parents while they shop. Yes, she had a three-year head start on my adjustment suggestion. My response finally was to build a world-class, fully staffed playground for children. McDonald's builds them right at the front of their stores. Now instead of dragging bored children along, customers can place them in the Gallery playground. Games, balls, puzzles, popcorn, cookies, and coloring sets are all available there for the children. Gallery now has a lot of smiling, happy kids playing, listening to music, and talking to each other while Mom and Dad shop around the store.

MACK LESSON

Kids Do Grow Up

In the retail business, children have to be considered because they accompany your customers. Turning a part of your business into a miniplayground will result in smiling children, laughter, fun, and repeat business. Customers who do not have to drag around crying, fidgeting children will want to come back again and again to shop. Also, remember these children will grow up and buy furniture themselves some day. If they like Gallery as 6-year-olds or 10-year-olds, they'll love Gallery when they are 35 years old.

Whatever goal or focus I am working on, I build in the possibility of making adjustments. I know that some adjustments are necessary to delight customers. I refuse to be hemmed in by rules or "you can't do this" statements. Rules are necessary, but sometimes they limit creativity and how a person thinks.

If what you're doing isn't working, try something else. Keep adjusting until you get what you want. A person will not fail until they run out of options. This should never happen unless you quit.

T = TENACITY

Think back to the last time you watched a baby attempting to walk. He or she takes a step and falls over and over again, never giving up. Babies want to walk and keep trying until they do walk or they become exhausted. The fourth element of my formula for building a positive attitude is tenacity. Being tenacious separates success from failure. When many people scoffed at my same-day delivery focus, plan, and schedule, I knew that some way I would make it happen. I was willing to pursue my plan until I succeeded.

I refuse to settle for less in anything I pursue. I believe that tenacity is more powerful than super intelligence, skill, and talent. The most gifted person, if he or she gives up, will finish behind the less gifted, tenacious person.

I believe that the most common reason we give up is that we no longer believe in what we are trying to accomplish. You must believe in what you are doing. Every day through my affirmation approach I believe in providing astonishing customer delight. I know that my work and effort is worthwhile after seeing a happy, loyal customer.

Unfortunately, tenacity is killed off in many people by fear. Fear usually is based on negative thinking. The more you focus on what is feared, the more likely it will occur. I learned about fear as a small boy. I hated receiving shots. My mother would coax me to the doctor's office, but I was in a state of fear. However, after a while, I learned that by focusing on what I wanted to be doing, playing baseball or throwing a football, my fear was reduced.

By playing in my mind something I wanted, instead of something I was trying to avoid, I had a better reaction. Not letting fear creep into my mental movies is now a regular routine. I persist without fear to accomplish what I want. I've found that picturing what I want makes me feel better and allows me to conquer fear. By conquering fear, I am able to focus, act, adjust, and persist. My four-part approach works again and helps me get what I want.

With tenacity, overcoming fear with positive thinking has become a habit of mine over the years. Once you quit the first time, it is easier the second time, and it becomes easier each additional time. Soon quitting becomes a habit. I refused to quit when I played football at the University of Texas and at North Texas State. I also refused to get out of business when my health club dream crumbled. Quitting as a habit was never given a chance.

My entrance into the television advertising world was filled with opportunities to quit. I couldn't get my lines straight, my hands moved all over the place, my eyes didn't look into the camera, and a hundred other flaws botched take after take. I had to redo these short commercials so many times I was exhausted. However, I needed to promote and sell Gallery Furniture. I refused to quit.

So many people have such a fear of failure that they never do anything risky. Once you set goals and focus on them, you are bound to have failures. I fail often. The best major league baseball batters fail seven out of ten times. They keep coming up to the plate to try again and again to succeed to get on base, drive in the run, or advance the base runner.

One major failure I experienced was when a number of furniture suppliers kept telling me to take a hike. They didn't want to do business with me. I searched and tried to understand the reason for all this rejection. My search was relentless. I talked to friends, suppliers who stayed with me, and suppliers who didn't want my business. Finally, my persistence paid off. I discovered that my driven style and my pushy approach to get it done now, alienated some people. My persistence resulted in a major adjustment in my approach to suppliers. I was a failure until I became determined to solve the problem. Some of what I found stung. Today, however, my persistence to solve any problems with suppliers is a model I use to study situations carefully so that I can make informed changes and decisions.

The important thing to remember is that failing is not the end unless you give up. Failing is one stop on the road to being successful. Slowing down or accepting failure are not part of my four-part approach. I increase my effort when faced with a setback. Persistence rules and spurs me on. It pushes me forward. It is a habit that will give you a chance to succeed.

Focus (F), action (A), search (S) for adjustments, and tenacity (T) are now daily habits that I have perfected. No one is born with these habits. Everyone must learn them. I refused to accept or be fearful of failure. With each new challenge I face, my first order of business is to use bite-size goals to focus better. By implementing FAST, you too can achieve what you want as a manager, entrepreneur, parent, husband, friend, or citizen.

5

Action before Energy

The first requisite for success is to apply your physical and mental energies to one problem incessantly without growing weary.

THOMAS EDISON

Becoming successful in business requires an enormous amount of energy. Why are some people energetic and some not? The answer comes down to having a very strong interest in or a passion for what you do. If you have that passion, you will be energized. I could do a lot of things in my life—jog, golf, go on long vacations—but I don't find these things interesting. When I do go on a vacation, I become bored and restless. I'm passionate about Gallery Furniture, serving customers, and solving the problems of the business. At Gallery I'm energized.

Success in life and in business requires that you have a big interest or a passion that draws out your natural energy. I have had many employees leave Gallery Furniture over the years to start their own furniture stores. Some of them have opened up right next

99

door or right down the block. None of them last long—I've even hired a few of them back. They don't last in business by themselves because they don't want to put in the time and energy required to be successful. You don't put in the time and won't have the energy if you lack passion. All successful persons that you meet have put in countless hours getting to where they are.

Most people envy the success but not the hard work. The successful person *enjoys* the success all the more *because* of the hard work it took to become successful.

Energy is not something a person has; it's something a person acquires. By being committed to my work, I become energized. My commitment means that I'm at the front of the store each day by 8:00 AM. It means that I'm still there at 11:00 PM making sure things are ready for the next day. Managers, business owners, and leaders are people who realize that energy comes from doing. I'm energized by being in the game. I don't wait to feel energized before getting into the action. If I did that, I'd be like a lot of other people who hit the snooze button when the alarm goes off at 6:00 in the morning. I don't feel energized until I'm on the Gallery floor making things happen. Do you see how this works? Energy is produced from doing rather than not doing.

Based on my own experiences and what I have observed in others, I believe there are four keys to developing high energy:

1. Leverage Your Strengths

2. Eliminate Distractions
3. Continuously Improve
4. Go with the Flow

LEVERAGE YOUR STRENGTHS

Everyone has interests. As we grow up, we naturally gravitate toward things that we do well and tend to drift away from those things we don't do well. Early in life, however, we're often told to spend more time on those things that we don't do well. Think about it. You remember those old school days when your teacher would make you spend hour after hour working on your penmanship, or your arithmetic, or something else, because you weren't as good at it as everyone else was. Meanwhile, those things you were good at were either emphasized less or neglected. What is the sense of that approach? On the one hand, you are forced to spend hours on something that you are not interested in; on the other, you probably aren't going to excel at something you have little talent for. It's no wonder some kids dislike school much of the time. Who wants to spend most of their time on things they don't enjoy?

I could spend every hour for the rest of my life in the gym and never be able to play basketball as well as Kobe Bryant of the Los Angeles Lakers. At the same time, even Kobe Bryant couldn't sell furniture as well and as consistently as I can. Kobe excels in basketball because he's a natural. I excel in selling furniture because I'm a natural at it.

Play with Abandon

When I played football, I would throw my body with reckless abandon into a fray that others wouldn't. It just didn't bother me to do that—to dive headlong into the pile. I always had that reputation. I wasn't the greatest player, but I did play recklessly. My strength was my ability to play with abandon, and that's how a small guy like me played college football. My energy came from the success I achieved by playing that way. The more my reputation for reckless play grew, the more energized I was to play even harder.

To be energized, you have to focus on those things that you do well and let go of those things you don't do well. You have to change the way you approach learning and career or business development. Although your school teachers should be honored and given thanks for all they taught you, one lesson they taught needs to be challenged and eliminated from your thinking, the lesson that you must spend more time working at what you don't do well.

The people in our world who have earned the greatest admiration and the greatest success excel at what they do. They spend hour upon hour working at and honing their skills. You know who they are; they appear in all walks of life. Some familiar names include Cal Ripken, Oprah Winfrey, and Steven Spielberg. Cal Ripken's dedication to refining his skills and keeping himself in shape enabled him to break the immortal

Lou Gehrig's "unbreakable" record for consecutive baseball games played. Oprah Winfrey is a master of communications. Her empire of television, publishing, and online business has made her one of the wealthiest self-made women of all time. Movie director Steven Spielberg is a master of the craft of movie making. I was involved in a movie project with Chuck Norris. We made a film called *Sidekicks*. I speak from experience when I tell you that making movies is extremely hard work because of the many details involved. Spielberg has three of the top ten grossing movies to his credit, and he's still working to improve. His dedication to the art of telling stories through film has made him one of the top movie directors of all time.

Each of these individuals has passion for what they do, and they are at their best when they leverage their strengths. Leveraging your strengths means, in part, having self-knowledge. You need to know what it is you're good at in order to focus on that skill and incrementally improve upon it every day. There's an easy way to do that. When I was coming out of my depression after having failed with the health clubs, I took stock of my assets and liabilities. You should do this as well on a regular basis, but let's change the language to *strengths* and *weaknesses*. Listing your strengths and weaknesses gives you a potent sense of who you are *right now*. And there's no better time to start changing your life than *right now*. Here's how to make your list.

Strengths	Weaknesses
1.	1.
2.	2.
3.	3.
4.	4.
5.	5.
6.	6.

Your strengths are those things that you do well. Your weaknesses are those things you don't do well. For example, on the strength side, you may list things like: big-picture thinker, good with numbers, or good with computers. On the weaknesses side, you might list things like: bad with details, impatient with customers, or poor at public speaking.

Once you have made your lists, study them for a while. Are there things you'd like to add? Anything you'd like to change? Now, here's the hard part. Show your lists to someone you trust, perhaps a business mentor or coach. Have them review your lists to determine whether they agree. Listen to their feedback. Do they agree that you are strong in the areas you think you're strong in? Do they think you have the weaknesses that you listed? Because getting feedback is a very important part of this exercise, don't shy away from it. Some of the feedback you get may surprise you.

Now that you have feedback, adjust and finalize your lists. This will result in fairly reliable lists of your strengths and weaknesses. The next step is to figure out how you are going to *leverage* your strengths and *compensate* for your weaknesses. Leveraging your strengths also means, in part, making full use of them. If your strength is that you are a big-picture thinker, then you need to find ways to practice this skill and contribute to the business. Big-picture thinkers are usually involved in strategic planning and upper management in organizations. They help the firm stay positioned for success in a dynamic environment. At the same time, big-picture types often aren't very good in operations. They become bored, lose track of details, and make careless mistakes. By knowing your strengths, you can find ways to leverage them to make the greatest contribution to your organization.

As for your weaknesses, you need to find some way to compensate for them. If you lack computer skills, for example, find a way around that problem. Don't spend time trying to be a computer scientist. Learn only what you need to get things done and then find other people or other ways to compensate for your lack of skill in that particular area. Face it, there's not enough time in anyone's life to master everything. It's your choice—in fact, it's your responsibility as a person, employee, and leader—to spend your time developing those skills that make you unique or distinguish you from everyone else. Distinguish yourself by your strengths.

At Gallery, we try to match people's strengths with their jobs, that is, we try to make sure that people work in an area that takes advantage of what they do particularly well. We don't try to make a silk purse out of a sow's ear, and we don't try to make a salesperson out of a truck driver. I firmly believe that each person has a unique gift, and the most rewarding thing I can do, as an employer, is to find a way to help each person express that gift in their work.

On Passion for Work

A lot of people are passionate about their hobbies and activities. My hobbies and activities are the business and its customers.

ELIMINATE DISTRACTIONS

I think the vast majority of people spend too much of their time in useless distractions and diversions. Don't get me wrong. I think people need diversions and recreation in order to have a balanced life. My worry is that we have created a world full of distractions, and most people allow the distractions to divert their attention from their personal goals. Distractions waste your time and energy.

Think about all the distractions that exist today: Sporting events, television, video games, the Internet, the telephone, cell phones, pagers, and the list goes on. Each of these distractions is harmless enough in themselves, but their collective impact can be devastating on an individual. How much time do you spend each day diverted by television programs, telephone calls, or by aimlessly surfing the Internet? Every minute that you spend in one of these activities—*every minute*—is a minute *not* spent leveraging your strengths and pursuing your goals.

A good way to find out how much extra time you can create for yourself by cutting back on distractions is to keep a daily log of your distractions for three days. Your log should be designed similar to the following:

Date_____

Distraction	**Time**	**Amount of Time**
Watching television	8:00 to 10:00 PM	2 hours

I realize it's a bit tedious—and even a bit distracting—for you to keep such a log. But it is designed to identify those activities that are your greatest time wasters. After you have done this for three days, examine your findings. Make categories such as:

Time spent watching television _____

Time spent surfing the Internet _____

Which category eats up the most of your valuable time? Are you surprised by your findings? You may have had an intuition going into this exercise about which of these distractions ate up the most of your time. Maybe you were surprised by the amount of time spent on distractions. Most people are a little surprised by how much time they waste. Now comes the hard part: Change. How do you change distraction time into useful, leverage-your-strength time? The answer is: Determination. You have to be determined to change how you spend your time. It's not easy. You have two things working against you: habit and laziness. I'm not saying you're lazy. It's just that most people are too lazy to want to change their habits. When you've fallen into a pattern of behavior over a period of years, the most difficult thing to do is generate the energy to change your pattern. I had to change my daily routines to work on this book. It wasn't easy, believe me. My coauthors and I got together many mornings when I wanted to be somewhere else. But we had a goal, and we were determined to get it done.

CONTINUOUSLY IMPROVE

Negative behavior must be changed. There are no two ways about it. If you are wasting energy on behaviors or emotions that are not helping you reach your goals, the energy wasters must be eliminated. If your business is not constantly and continuously improving, it is becoming lethargic and stale.

One of the most energizing pieces of advice that came out of the quality movement, discussed in more detail in Chapter 7, is that businesses should strive for continuous improvement. This idea suggests that work is never done, that higher levels of quality and customer delight can always be reached. I love this concept and truly believe that it has made a huge difference for Gallery Furniture. The idea of continuous improvement helps us avoid the lurching changes that fad-of-the-month gurus constantly tout. We don't go in for re-engineering, or downsizing, or any of the other fads. We strive to improve constantly and steadily.

Most lasting change in life and business happens a little bit at a time. Only constant attention to your actions and their outcomes over a period of time will produce lasting change. Think about it. Most of us know someone who has tried to diet or to quit smoking. What's the typical behavior pattern they go through? Most will make a commitment to change. The first day is fairly easy—they are vigilant about their behavior and control their urges to eat or to smoke. As time goes on, however, they get less vigilant. They allow themselves a snack or a cigarette break that they know is contrary to their long-range goal. Soon enough, they're back to their old pattern of eating or smoking. No lasting change has occurred. They get angry with themselves for being weak, and they often refuse to make any further attempts to change. It's a familiar and tragic behavior pattern.

Every business has the ability to continuously improve, but it takes determination to monitor old behaviors until the new behavior takes hold. How can you do that? I have used a technique over the years that I find to be particularly effective. When I want to make a change in a behavior, I break it up into manageable, bite-sized chunks. Then, I monitor my behavior in each of those small chunks to make sure it is in line with my long-term goals. For example, when I was trying to change my tendency toward getting angry over bad news, I did it in chunks of 30 minutes for 3 days. Each 30 minutes during those 3 days I asked myself if I was behaving the way I wanted. If not, I would change it.

Let me tell you, it was very difficult to ask myself that question every 30 minutes for 3 days. Many times I was swamped with other issues and problems. But I was determined to change, and I knew I had to overcome a long history of reacting in an angry manner when an employee brought bad news to light. I caught myself getting angry many times and immediately changed my behavior to be more in line with what was needed to be successful with my business.

After those first 3 days, I monitored my behavior every 60 minutes for another day. The day after that, it was every 120 minutes. Soon enough, I was catching my tantrums before they began, and my new behavior pattern started to take on a life of its own. The new behavior became a new habit, and I no longer had to pay as much attention as I did during the change process. Of course, human nature being what it is, I'm still not perfect. But I am a lot better than I used to be, and that's an achievement. My business is certainly better off now that I am able to receive bad news unemotionally.

GO WITH THE FLOW

I think it was the late John Lennon who said that life is what happens while you're busy making other plans. Anyone who has lived long enough will realize that there are just too many things beyond a person's control to make exacting plans. At Gallery, we've never had a formal business plan. That doesn't mean I'm not organized, or that I just do whatever I want when the mood hits me. I believe some of the most profitable opportunities are those that appear unexpectedly. If they fit with the business's long-term goals, these opportunities can be added to the firm's portfolio of projects. While you want to guard against distractions—as we've already learned—you want to go with the flow when interesting and related projects come along.

MACK SPEAK

Don't Be Impulsive

I used to be terribly impulsive. That's how I got into the movie business. I met Chuck Norris, and we made Sidekicks *together. The movie didn't make much money in the United States, but it did very well overseas. After all was said and done, we made money with the movie, but we had to work very hard at it. I impulsively jumped into movie making without looking at all of the costs and challenges.*

In the year 2000, I was approached by a group that wanted to bring a college football bowl game back to

Houston. It didn't take me long to decide to get involved in that. I know football, and I know that Houston is a football town. I also knew there were some risks, and I knew there would be some naysayers. But I believed the bowl game would blend nicely with Gallery's general sports marketing theme. The first bowl game was held on December 28, 2000. While the attendance was less than I had planned, the game was a success. The second game was held on December 28, 2001, featuring Texas A&M University versus Texas Christian University. My ability to go with the flow enabled me to fit the bowl game and all of the work involved with that into Gallery's other sports marketing events, including:

- Hosting the Men's Clay Court Tennis Championship at Gallery's West Side Tennis Club
- Hosting a holiday basketball tournament at the University of Houston
- Sponsoring the World Wrestling Foundation Wrestlemania XVII
- Building and maintaining the practice facilities for the Houston Rockets of the NBA and Houston Comets of the WNBA

Going with the flow means integrating new business and marketing opportunities into your existing portfolio. For me, that often means opportunities to spread the Gallery message through speeches and other public appearances. I now do over 300 speeches each year to all kinds of people—from elementary school kids to television executives. Opportunities to speak and spread the Gallery message come in every day. Oddly, I'm an introverted person by nature, but I enjoy speaking about Gallery and our great work here.

Giving speeches isn't easy, but I go with the flow because I know that speaking events help build the Gallery brand. Sometimes, going with the flow means being resourceful and determined. Probably my best example of going with the flow involves a major speech I made at the International Quality and Services Convention at the University of Karlstad, in Karlstad, Sweden. People involved in research concerning customer service were there from around the world. A lot of academics, business people, and other high-level officials attended.

I traveled to Sweden with my wife Linda, my assistant, James, and an entourage of about a dozen people, including my children and some of their friends. Because we intended to spend two weeks in Sweden, we packed lots of bags. Unfortunately, the reservations that we made were a little bit fuzzy. We landed in Stockholm, Sweden, and we were supposed to be met by a person with a placard that said, "McIngvale." Well, when we landed we found no one there to meet us. I thought, "No problem, I'll just go rent a car." James and I left Linda and the kids at the airport and went to rent a car. Unfortunately, we were told no cars were available because of a convention in town.

When we returned to the group, Linda informed us she had called the hotel and—you guessed it—the reservations were messed up. For some reason, the hotel had canceled our reservations, and no rooms were available because of the convention.

Things were not looking good. On top of all of these problems, it was very cold in Stockholm and we were all getting hungry after the long trip. I had to be in Karlstad, some 300 miles away, at 10:30 the next morning to give the speech. You simply can't crumble in such a situation. You have to find a way. You have to work at solving the problem. We decided to grab a bus and head for downtown Stockholm. I had my cell phone, so I called my assistant in Houston and told him to get on the Internet and find a hotel that had rooms available. By the time we arrived downtown, it was about 6:00 PM, the wind was blowing hard, and it was very cold. Finally, my assistant called me on the cell phone and told me he had found one room in a nearby hotel.

Because the available accommodation was a suite, it was acceptable to us. But it was very tight. Luckily, James and I were planning to go to Karlstad that night by train so we didn't need to stay in the room.

After checking into the hotel room, the kids wanted to go to get something to eat. So we left the hotel in two taxicabs to go to the restaurant. James and I had our bags packed to go from the restaurant directly to the train station. We were sitting there eating and, about halfway through the meal, James shouted, "Oh no!" I said, "What in God's name is it now?" James stared at me with a stunned look on his face and blurted out that he had left our computer with the speech on it in the taxi.

Without that computer, I didn't have a speech for the several hundred people who were waiting to hear me the next day. So James went to call the cab company, but I said: "Just forget that. There are 5,000 cabs in town. You aren't going to find that computer tonight." We walked out of the restaurant, and right next door was a 7-Eleven. I went into the 7-Eleven, bought a yellow pad, and said, "Come on, James. I'm not going to holler and scream at you. The milk's been spilled. Let's go to the meeting. I'll just rewrite the speech in longhand, and I'll make it through."

After saying our goodbyes to the rest of the group, James and I got in another taxi and went to the train station. Once there, we learned the train to Karlstad had been canceled.

Let's pause here to take stock of the situation. It's 10:00 at night, I have no speech, I'm 300 miles from my destination, and I have to be in Karlstad to speak at 10:30 the next morning. To make matters worse, the computer that held my speech and slides was in a taxi somewhere in Stockholm. James and I went outside and found the newest taxi we could find. We ended up with a Volvo station wagon; a brand-new-looking car. I said to the driver: "You've got to take us to Karlstad." He said, "Too far, too far." So I pulled out a wad of money, and he said, "Get in."

We finally set out for Karlstad at about 10:30 PM, 12 hours before my scheduled speech. We were driving into the dark Swedish night and had gotten about 50 miles outside of Stockholm when the cell phone rang. It was Linda, calling from the hotel in Stockholm. She informed me that they had called the taxicab company and that they had found the computer. I knew the speech would be better if I had the computer, so I told our taxi driver to turn around and go back to Stockholm so we could pick it up. So we drove back to Stockholm, picked up the computer, and set out once more for Karlstad. It was now past 1:00 AM, less than ten hours to my speech.

I fell asleep in the back of the taxi as we made our way through the cold, dark night. At about 3:30 AM, as we were approaching Karlstad, I was awakened by the taxi driver's screaming and cursing in Swedish. It seems that the car immediately in front of us had just smashed into a thousand-pound moose that had been standing in the road. The moose and the car were all over the road, but we somehow managed to maneuver around them and arrived in Karlstad in time to make the speech.

The moral of this story is simple: Adapting on the fly and adjusting to the situation are necessary to keep your energy flowing. If you are easily knocked off course by distractions or obstacles, or by failure, you won't be able to sustain a high energy level. When people get off course they get bored, depressed, or frustrated. These are energy sapping emotions. I believe it all traces back to how you feel about yourself. The more certain you are of your goals and the more *determined* you are to reach them come what may, the better you feel about yourself.

On Moving Past Failure

We tried selling furniture on the Internet for a while. At the time, a lot of hype was circulating about how big the Internet was going to be and how everyone was going online to buy consumer goods. So we built a Web site and found out pretty quickly that we couldn't make money selling a couch to a family in Boston. I realized pretty fast that selling furniture online wasn't going to work for us. I pulled the plug on the venture after three or four months and after investing several hundred thousand dollars. I didn't look back. We tried selling on the Internet, and it didn't work. NEXT!

It's never easy. If I had a dollar for each Friday night we had to stay open late to sell one more piece of furniture so that we could make payroll, I could buy one of Gallery's big-screen TVs. Going with the flow means accepting the way things are without giving up your attempts to change things. Business will always present problems. Nobody that I know has had everything work out the way they wanted it to work out. Every business faces obstacles, problems, and challenges.

It takes courage to stay the course, work the problem, and retain your high level of energy. When you really think about it though, what choice do you have?

You can take on the challenge, or you can shy from it, wondering what might have been. The correct choice seems obvious.

FINAL THOUGHTS

I like positive thinking. Over the years, I have read many books, listened to many tapes, and attended many seminars on the power of positive thinking. I'm a big believer in the concept that the way you think determines the way you feel. I want to feel energized and enthusiastic, so I need to think that way. Many people make their living by giving motivational speeches to large groups. Tony Robbins, for example, motivates thousands of people each year through mass meetings that resemble religious revivals. I have had the opportunity to meet Tony and to speak at a few of his events. Let me tell you, he really gets people excited.

How can Tony make a living by giving motivational speeches? I'll tell you how. His system works: People actually do get energized and take positive action for themselves and their companies after listening to motivational speakers like Tony. The positive talk they hear and the stories of success that they listen to are inspirational. I'll bet a lot of people reading this book have at some point in their lives watched the original *Rocky* movie starring Sylvester Stallone. Who could possibly watch that movie and not feel motivated? The story of the unknown boxer who gets a chance at a title fight and makes the best of his chance through hard work and dedication is an American classic. Americans love the underdog. They love stories about the little guy beating the big guy. Well, envision yourself and your business to be the little guy against the world. You are the underdog, and you have to dig deep into yourself to find the spirit to win.

MACK CASE

Notre Dame

Motivational ideas and positive messages can help you tap into your winning spirit. There are a number of ways that you can expose yourself to these ideas and messages. Football teams, such as Notre Dame, have messages about the rich tradition and the privilege of being a member of the Fighting Irish posted throughout their practice facility and locker room. Playing football for Notre Dame is an honor, tradition, and responsibility that is very energizing. The long history of success enjoyed by the Notre Dame football program is in part attributable to the tremendous effort each player gives because they are energized by the messages, images, and symbols of success that surround them.

There are a lot of different audiotapes, videotapes, books, Internet Web sites, and posters you can use to maintain a positive frame of mind.

I won't endorse any one of these motivational resources or any particular motivational speaker or author. Everyone has a different message and a different way of delivering their message. You should probably read or listen to a number of different motivational experts. Not a single one of them has a perfect or timeless message. As progress is made in knowledge of human nature and its capabilities, the motivational messages change. The crucial point is this: Who you read or listen to is less important than the positive, life-affirming messages and ideas they provide.

As the leader of Gallery Furniture, I have to maintain a positive disposition. Employees watch their leaders to determine their own mood. I know they watch me. In fact, they used to play a little trick to let everyone know when I was on the store property. When anyone spotted my car arriving in the parking lot, they would pick up the nearest public address microphone and announce, "Elvis is on the lot." This was a coded message to all employees that I was on the premises.

Unfortunately, at the time, the message was more of a warning. When that tactic was being used, Gallery was still using commissioned sales, and I ruled like a tyrant. Of course, we've changed all that, but employees still watch me for signs of distress or concern. I have learned that my disposition sets the tone for the entire business. If I'm positive, optimistic, and enthusiastic, then so is everyone else. As the leader, I accept the responsibility to establish the mood of the organization. A positive mood promotes customers being served and furniture moving out the door. A negative mood leads to customer neglect, lost sales, and mistakes.

In addition to being positive, I find it to be helpful to be focused on the future. I don't like to live in the past. I live by the belief that *what's done is done.* If I can't fix something that I've messed up, I don't spend time with it. I move on. I don't allow myself to feel guilty or to be encumbered by the past. Again, that may sound crass or unfeeling, but if I can't do something about what's been done, I don't worry about it. Why should I? If I make a mistake or hurt someone, I feel bad about it like everyone else. But if I can't fix it, I don't see the point in worrying about it or feeling guilty about it. I do try to learn from it. I do try to not repeat a mistake or any offensive behavior. But I refuse to spend a single moment of my time in useless guilt or self-pity.

It's easy for me to talk about energy—I've always had it. There's no doubt in my mind that energetic people are made and not born. A high-energy level comes from being active, doing things, enjoying small victories. Most people think that you need energy to take action. But the opposite is the case. Taking action creates the energy.

People who sit around waiting for a bolt of energy to hit them so they can get up and take action will be waiting a long time. Believe me, I've been there and I know. You have to get up and do something. Often, you might not feel like it. In fact, you may feel like not doing anything at all. That's what depression is. Don't let negative emotions rule your life. Take action. Get energized.

6

Sell with Pride

Try not to become a man of success, but rather to become a man of value.

ALBERT EINSTEIN

What I do for a living gives me an enormous sense of pride. What could be more important than making a sale? I don't know who said, "Nothing happens in business until a sale is made," but they were right. I would go so far as to say, "Nothing happens in life until a sale is made."

Selling is something we all do, all the time. To get someone to do something, you have to sell them on your idea. You have to help them create a mental image, a feeling that they will be better off by taking the course of action you recommend. That's what all good salespeople do. Whether it's selling furniture at Gallery, selling insurance, or selling cars, you have to help customers *see* and *feel* the benefits of taking your recommended action. All good salespeople create an image of a better life for customers—however small the

123

improvement might be. Anyone involved in helping people create and achieve their dreams should feel a sense of immense pride.

The most successful brands have always associated themselves with good feelings and positive emotions. Look at the cola wars, for example. The major brands stumble over each other trying to prove that they will make you feel good. Leading brands sell products and services of high quality, but they also sell by appealing to basic human emotions. Gallery has done this from the very start. We knew people get frustrated with traditional furniture stores, backorder slips, and sloppy service. Gallery has created a sustainable advantage around its ability to help customers avoid frustrating backorders. We offer quality products and great services, but we also help people feel good.

Selling with pride means two things to Gallery: Be aggressive about building a brand and be systematic about selling. Pride in selling means being proud of your brand and its image. We are aggressive in building our brand because we want everyone to know about us and check us out. Pride in selling also means being serious about the sales process. To us, selling is a science that can be analyzed, tested, and constantly improved. We want each Gallery salesperson to consistently exceed customers' expectations.

BUILD THE BRAND

My television commercials are known throughout the United States for their tackiness and simplicity. Gallery's commercials have been featured on NBC's *Late Night with Conan O'Brien* as being the "worst" in the land. I don't mind. I know that Gallery's commercials work—they get people into our store. I personally am involved in every television spot. If I'm not in the commercial itself, then I'm doing the voice-over. I want people to be comfortable with the Gallery brand and with me. "Mattress Mack" and "Gallery" are one-and-the-same.

I'll grant that my commercials are not polished and market tested. Generally, they feature me jumping, shouting, and pounding on "solid-wood" furniture, and they end with me exclaiming, "Gallery Furniture Saves You Money." Our brand is built through a constant stream of television, radio, billboard, and print ads. Gallery is consistently sited as the most well-known brand in the region. A lot of retailers are reluctant to spend much of their hard-earned cash on advertising because it uses money resources today to try to create more money resources tomorrow. It's a risky proposition when your cash is tight and when there are no guarantees for a return. We decided long ago that we were going to build the Gallery brand and spend as much as needed to create a presence in this market like no other. We've done that through advertising. Whoever said, "Early to bed and early to rise, work like heck and advertise!" was right. It works!

When I learned of the power of advertising, I made a huge commitment to it. Early on, we poured nearly every dollar of profit into advertising. At first, all we could afford were tiny classified ads, but they had a powerful effect. The more we advertised, the more I became convinced of the necessity of building and protecting the brand.

Today, Gallery spends nearly 30 percent of its gross profit on advertising. You can't spend a single day in Southeast Texas without hearing or seeing a Gallery ad. In fact, if you tuned around the radio dial at any give time, you'd probably come across a Gallery ad within a few minutes. We run hundreds of spots per day on radio.

Gallery's brand building also uses a sports marketing approach. This has been very successful for us. We have spent a lot of money to be associated with sporting events and with sports personalities. The link to sports gives Gallery an aura of energy and vitality. It also links us to the community and helps us become more visible to the many sports fans in the region.

Sports marketing can work for nearly anyone. Don't be fooled into thinking that it takes a lot of money to get involved with athletes and professional sports teams. I do spend a lot of money on sports marketing today, but I didn't spend much to get started. For example, many lesser-known athletes who don't get a lot of endorsement opportunities will be willing to work for low fees or even on a commission basis.

Former pros or pros who are currently not well known are often delighted to get opportunities to be in the limelight. That's how I got started. It wasn't long before I was working with the superstars, like Andre Agassi, Shaquille O'Neal, Clyde Drexler, Brandi Chastain, Mary Lou Retton, and Bela Karolyi.

The sports marketing approach can build over time if you give back to the athletes and teams that you work with. Gallery did this by building practice facilities for the Houston Rockets of the NBA and the Houston Comets of the WNBA. Now, every time one of the Rockets or Comets is interviewed at practice, the Gallery logo is in the background getting air time that was not billed to the advertising account.

MACK SPEAK

My Publicity Stunts

I enjoy creating new ways to promote Gallery. Some of the things I've been involved in over the years include:

- *Wrestling "Stone Cold" Steve Austin for charity prior to Wrestlemania XVII*
- *Shaving my head to promote the Houston Rockets NBA Finals appearance*
- *Giving more than 4,500 speeches in the past 15 years*
- *Sponsoring and organizing an annual Thanksgiving Feast for thousands of people at Houston's George R. Brown Convention Center*

- *Purchasing the Grand Champion steer for $670,000 at the Houston Livestock Show and Rodeo*
- *Sparring with Muhammad Ali*

SALES PROFESSIONALISM

Professionalism in selling is very important to Gallery. Of course, the meaning of that term has changed over time. I used to think that professional selling meant putting it all on the line, working for straight commission, do or die—just like my Dad used to do. If you look back to the early days of Gallery, you'd find a frantic group of salespeople trying very hard to meet their sales quotas. Customers would walk in the front door and immediately be confronted by a small army of salespeople. We didn't pay attention to who the customer was. If it was your turn in the rotation, you were the salesperson who waited on that customer.

In the early days, Gallery salespeople worked on straight commission. To make things even more intense, we set our sales goals very high. People who didn't commit to working long hours were just not going to make it. In those days, professionalism to me meant selling on commission, working long hours, doing whatever was necessary to make a sale, and being motivated by money.

I don't think that way anymore. In Chapter 3, I told you about my efforts in the early 1990s to adopt the Deming approach to total quality management

(TQM). I went to Deming seminars all over the country. I was fascinated by Dr. Deming's business philosophy, and I asked a lot of questions. He kept telling me the same things over and over—and while I was hearing him, I just wasn't listening. Linda had raced ahead of me and was making remarkable progress with TQM in the warehouse. She kept badgering me to make the same commitment to change the Gallery approach to sales, but there was one part of Deming's teachings that I just couldn't put into practice—he told me to take all Gallery's salespeople off commission and put them on salary.

That was something I just couldn't do. Selling on commission was how my Dad had done it, it was how I had done it, and to me it was the essence of professionalism. But you can't do TQM halfway. You can't get healthy unless you take all the medicine. My tinkering with TQM and leaving the selling process unchanged was not helping Gallery reach the goals we had set. Finally one Sunday night, Linda told me it was time to stop procrastinating. She said I either had to adopt TQM all the way and change the Gallery selling process, or I had to resign myself to the way things were. I couldn't possibly accept the stand-still option. So, the next morning I called all the salespeople together and told them that we were going off commission selling. From that point on, everyone would be paid a salary, and we would all share in the company's growth at the end of each quarter.

Change Is Never Easy

When Gallery first changed to total quality management (TQM), neither the salespeople nor I knew what was going to happen. A few of the top sellers absolutely resisted becoming salaried salespeople. They were making a lot of money on commission and feared they would make less under the new system. I had to answer a lot of questions during the first few days. People had to adjust their thinking and their goals.

All businesses have trouble making system-wide change. People fear for their jobs, their paychecks, and their security. Leaders must be reassuring, supportive, and yet firm enough to create system-wide change. We eventually successfully accepted TQM, including salaried salespeople, and we've never looked back.

It wasn't long before people realized improvements in working conditions as a result of the new, salaried approach. It took me even less time to realize that I had made the right decision. Today, I can't imagine any other compensation system. Today, everyone at Gallery is focused on taking care of customers. They're not in the back somewhere figuring how much money they made on their last sale. There is no incentive to mislead customers because a salesperson has to make a car payment tomorrow. All those bad things are out, and the system works better. We do have to manage more because some people may lose their focus during the 12-hour days, but that's part of the TQM philosophy. As Dr. Deming put it, "That's the job of the manager."

Under the Deming or TQM approach, managers are responsible for establishing a business system under which people can be successful. The job of the manager is to set up the system and then let people take pride in their ability to achieve their goals within that framework. Unsuccessful managers make the mistake of constantly intervening or, as Deming put it, "tampering" with the system. Tampering pushes the system out of balance and creates wide fluctuations in quality. At Gallery we have established a system, a framework, in which people are encouraged to use their talents to achieve their goals. We don't hover and judge. We don't command and control. We do monitor overall performance based on revenue, profit, and units sold. If these numbers are on target and Gallery's customers are reporting satisfaction, then we have done our job.

MACK LESSON

Some Things about Selling Never Change

My perspective on sales professionalism has definitely changed over time. But some things haven't changed. Professionalism in selling still means hard work and long hours. It still means knowing your product and setting goals. What I have learned is that the essence of professionalism in selling is delighting the customer.

SELLING IS A SYSTEM

It's very important to think of selling as a system. Somebody once asked me if selling is an art or a science. Most people like to think it's an art. They think that being glib or being attractive are the keys to making a sale. While these may be important ingredients in selling, they won't translate to long-term, consistent selling success. To achieve that—and anyone who's in business will tell you that repeat sales are very desirable—you have to make selling a system, a science.

We are very systematic about selling at Gallery, beginning with training. For example, every Wednesday and Thursday, our sales managers gather our salespeople together from 8:00 AM to 11:00 AM to discuss sales techniques and strategy. These sessions include a lot of role-playing and situational analysis. The sales team goes through a range of scenarios that start with "If this happened to me, how would I deal with it?" We do more sales training than probably any furniture store in the country. I believe it pays off in the way we treat our customers. To me, being nice to people—being professional—is second nature. However, the concept of delighting customers is not second nature to many of the salespeople that we hire. So we train them and train them and train them until they understand. Then, we train them some more.

We weren't always so systematic. Selling at Gallery used to be a slam, bam affair. When a customer came in, the next salesperson in line took that customer no matter who they were. The salesperson followed the customer around the whole store, trying to sell them every item. After the customer left, the salesperson went to the end of the line and waited his or her turn again.

Today, Gallery sales associates work in different areas of the store using a process we call "Zone Selling." Some people specialize in recliners, some in wood furniture, others in home office, and still others in bedding. On weekends, holidays, and other busy days when a customer comes in, they are welcomed to Gallery by an individual "greeter." The greeter has been trained to ask questions to find out if the customer has been to Gallery before, what type of furniture they're looking for, and if there's anything else they need. The greeter answers all questions and personally *escorts* the customer to their desired area of the store. The greeter lets the customer know how to contact a salesperson if they need one and that they can approach *any* Gallery employee if they have a question. Our salespeople have been trained to be helpful but not aggressive with customers.

On weekdays, when customer traffic is lighter, we don't use the zone selling approach as much. Rather, we use an approach that we call "Mirror Matching." With this approach, we assign different salespeople to different types of people. For example, if a Spanish-speaking customer comes into the store, a Spanish-speaking salesperson will wait on them. If it's an older woman looking for a power recliner, we get an older person to wait on her. Mirror matching has been very successful for us, increasing weekday sales by about 20 percent.

This systematic approach to selling is further enhanced by our overall sales system. We have a routine way of greeting customers, getting to know a little bit about them, informing them about Gallery and the furniture we stock, and helping them make a buying decision that fits their needs. When customers come to Gallery today, they get a very consistent experience no matter who their salesperson happens to be. This systematic and consistent technique has created an extremely high volume of repeat customers. In our business, we want people coming back to Gallery throughout their lifetimes to meet their changing furniture needs. If they are comfortable with our people and satisfied with our furniture, they'll come back. Why would they want to go somewhere else and have to deal with a completely different approach and experience?

Customer loyalty is one way we keep track of how we're doing with our selling system. If customers receive the value we promise, they will come back for more, tell others, and serve as our indirect sales team. Achieving customer loyalty is a top priority in our efforts to systematize the Gallery selling process.

Customers Crave Consistency

If there's one thing that I've learned in my years of selling furniture, it's that people want to feel comfortable with their buying decision. At Gallery, we help people understand their purchase, feel comfortable with it, and ensure that it's in their home and making them happy before the day is done.

Everyone at Gallery is trained in selling and in the selling system. Because customers are unpredictable, everyone in the store needs to be ready to help solve customer problems. Gallery will simply not lose a sale because the customer couldn't find someone to help them. At worst, they will come to the front desk where the receptionist will answer their questions and, if possible, close the sale.

I remember an auto dealer who had about ten salespeople in the showroom. One day, it was raining so there weren't many customers coming in. All the salespeople were in a backroom somewhere playing cards. They weren't paying attention to an older-looking gentleman who drove up and was looking at a few cars. The dealership's finance manager happened to be out on the lot looking for a car that he couldn't find in the inventory. The older gentleman who had been on the lot flagged him down and asked him if he could look at a new car. The finance manager said "sure" and opened the door of the car the man was looking at.

Immediately the old guy jumped into the backseat and lay down. The finance manager thought the guy might be nuts. But seconds later, the gentlemen got out and stated that he was an oil man and had to visit a number of rigs around the country. While he was on the road, he liked to catch naps in the backseat of his car so it had to be large enough to accommodate him. That finance manager soon learned what it means to be in the right place at the right time. The oilman liked the car so much he bought 35 of them—on the spot. It would have been a shame if the finance manager had not been trained to take care of that customer.

MOTIVES FOR SELLING

People use many motives to help them be successful in sales. For example, everyone knows that salespeople are motivated by money. Who isn't? But it's always amazed me that people think of salespeople as being *primarily* motivated by money.

Let's put an end to that myth right here. Salespeople are no more money motivated than the guy on the Ford assembly line, or the woman who owns a restaurant, or the person who manages a mutual fund, or the doctor or lawyer. They *all* want to make money. So let's end the nonsense that salespeople are *uniquely* money motivated. Every profession or job is at least partly about making money. How else would a person survive in a free-enterprise society? Putting a label on salespeople as being solely money motivated is simply inaccurate.

Gallery wants all its salespeople to be money motivated in the sense that we want them to be proud of their work, do a good job, and support their families. However, we have found that a far more potent motivator behind successful selling is a genuine desire to help other people. I have been in this business for more than 25 years, and I have seen all kinds of salespeople come and go. The ones that stay the longest, enjoy their work the most, and, usually, make the most money, are those who truly enjoy making other people happy.

First-time customers come into Gallery Furniture every day. They're unsure about what they're about to experience. They've probably seen us on television or heard Gallery ads on the radio and are curious about our unique store. They are here as much to learn about the Gallery mystique as they are to purchase furniture. What do you think would happen to these people if we applied the old hard-sell approach? You're right. They would be turned off and probably never return. What do we do instead? We treat them to hot cookies baking fragrantly in ovens located throughout the store. We greet them and help them find the area of the store they're looking for. If they have kids, we ask if they'd like to let the kids play for free in our on-site day care. If they're elderly and have trouble walking, we ask them if they'd like to borrow a free motorized scooter. They can stop by our four-lane bowling alley, gaze at Shaquille O'Neal's oversized sneakers, see Elvis Presley's car, or marvel at Princess Diana's jewelry. Gallery is set up to entertain and delight customers. Gallery salespeople are motivated by helping people.

Shopping at Gallery is an experience. We hire salespeople who are motivated to help customers enjoy their experience. We have people who specialize in telling jokes. We have others who specialize in lashing furniture to cars, trucks, and other moving objects so customers can get their new furniture home quickly. We don't take tips, and we don't sell something that the customer doesn't want. Our staff members are focused on delighting customers, and they are motivated by that. There is nothing sweeter for me, as the owner, than to see sales associates and customers enjoying themselves as they experience everything Gallery has to offer. I'll catch myself watching the customers and their smiling faces and feel a genuine sense of pride and satisfaction. We've created a destination—a place where people come to just to feel good. The better they feel about Gallery, me, and our entire team, the better they'll feel about coming back again and again. Look, people need furniture and are going to buy it somewhere. Gallery creates an environment where people are comfortable to make their buying decision. *Our primary motive is to make people happy.* The more we focus on that motivation, the more money we make.

With this approach, our sales associates are always on the floor with customers. Gallery doesn't even have computer terminals on the floor for the salespeople. Do you want to know why? If we had computer terminals on the floor, some salespeople would spend all day in front of the computer. You see, the computer can't tell them "no." The computer can't tell them "Your prices are too high." It can't tell them "You stink." But customers can, and they will. The customers will tell you exactly how they feel. Gallery wants its sales associates to stay eyeball-to-eyeball, face-to-face, nose-to-nose with the customers all of the time. That's how we create value and an enjoyable experience for customers.

MACK SPEAK

Stark Raving Fans

Our goal at Gallery is to delight customers to the point where they would never even consider going anywhere else. We want to make them stark raving fans. Once you do that, price is not the issue. I have a relationship with Southwestern Bell because one of our guy's wives has worked there for 20 years. If we ever have a problem on the telephone, he calls her and she fixes it in two minutes. I don't care what Bell's rates are. Other companies' salespeople come in all the time wanting to lowball those rates, but it doesn't matter. Southwestern Bell has got me for life because they have that great service. That's the ultimate goal—to please those customers so much they won't think of going anywhere else. If you merely satisfy them, all they are going to do is price shop.

GOALS, NOT QUOTAS

Success in selling requires setting and achieving goals. The very definition of success makes this obvious. If you achieve your goals, you are successful. A lot of people have forgotten that success is linked to goals. They see someone who drives a nice car or works for a fancy company, and they say that the person is successful. They see the fancy car or the nice office; they don't see the hard work and goal setting that preceded the rewards.

I don't know a single successful person who has not had to go through difficult times to reach success. Every entrepreneur that I know has had many trying times where the path to success was not clear or obvious. Of course, I've experienced that in my own life. Many times I've been unsure about what to do about a problem or issue. Many times I've tossed and turned late into the night as I mulled over a problem from every possible angle searching for a solution. That's the price of having goals. If you have goals, it becomes a habit for you to do whatever is necessary to achieve them.

How do you set goals? Most people don't set their own goals. Their company sets their goals for them. They are required to sell so many pieces of furniture, or they're required to write so many column inches of newspaper stories, or they are supposed to process so many cubic feet of natural gas. These are goals that are imposed from *external* sources. They are important, and they occupy a great deal of time for most everyone.

But goals can also be set *internally,* and these are the goals that take the rare individual to greater heights. Think about it, if you spend your whole life pursuing and achieving the goals that have been set by others— external goals— you will probably be viewed as a very valuable employee. You will be someone who is reliable, and you're likely to get promotions on your way up the corporate ladder. But if your whole perspective is to achieve the goals that others have set, you will never break out of the box. You will define success only as achieving those *external* goals.

No company can aspire to greatness that doesn't have people who set and achieve their own internal goals. At Gallery, people who acted above and beyond the call of duty attained some of our greatest achievements. They acted on their own sense of purpose, their own set of values, and their own internally established goals.

We set up sales goals for the entire company. At Gallery, it's up to the individual to set his or her own personal sales targets. We provide each person with the support they need to reach whatever sales goals they decide are appropriate for them. We don't do traditional "performance reviews." People are evaluated solely by their results against the goals they set. Individuals who don't set high enough goals won't achieve personal satisfaction working at Gallery. The salaries we provide are adequate to pay some of their bills, but people need to work hard to drive Gallery's profits and thus share in its success. They have to decide for themselves that they will work ten hours instead of eight hours, six days instead of five days, and whether they are going to gather their internal resources to greet one more customer each and every day.

How does the individual set *internal* goals? It's a complicated question because each individual has to set goals in a unique way. Everyone should set goals that are consistent with his or her values, personality, knowledge, and skills. Don't set as your goal, for example, to be a movie star, if you have no knowledge of the industry or don't have good acting skills. On the other hand, be careful not to limit your goals based on your *current* knowledge and skills. You could always learn how to be a good actor, for example. A good goal takes into account a realistic assessment of your current skill set, the likelihood of being able to develop it, and the length of time that would be required to get where you want to be.

Goal setting is systematic. To set your own internal goals, make sure that you pay attention to:

- *The clarity of your goals.* Goals should be able to be stated or written clearly in one or two sentences. For example, a good goal statement is: "Sell $100,000 worth of furniture." A poorly worded goal statement is: "Sell furniture." The first one is clear and provides a measure for success. The second has no clear endpoint and is not measurable.

- *The timeframe of your goals.* Make sure you allow enough time to achieve your goals. Setting unreasonable time limits on yourself will lead to frustration, stress, and giving up. Goals take time, usually more time than we estimate. Always set goals with the assumption that they will take more time to reach than you think. If you want to sell $100,000 worth of furniture in two weeks, assume it will take a month. Then, go for it.

- *The value of your goals.* Don't bother setting goals that are generalities. For example, don't set a goal to be a "good" salesperson. Setting general goals will waste your limited amount of mental attention. Set goals on big things, life changing things, and important things. Don't set a goal to become a "top" salesperson but set one to achieve a definitive percentage increase in sales, say 20 percent per month. Set specific goals that are important and worthy of your attention.

These three elements of goal setting will help you focus on the things that are important in your life. They will also help you develop a framework for continuous success. A wise person once said that success is a journey not a destination. By setting goals you will experience a constant stream of successes (and some failures) on your journey. Without goals, life is simply aimless wandering. With goals, you define who you are, what's important to you, and where you want to go.

If you are not familiar with setting goals, try setting a few small ones before you tackle the really big ones. Try losing two pounds before you lose ten pounds. Try running a quarter mile before you run a mile. You will have a lot more fun with goal setting if you set goals that are reasonably challenging. Success breeds success. As you achieve the small goals, you will feel confident and energized to begin taking on bigger challenges. Start small, and then Think Big.

Big things do not come from small thinkers. I believe the American economy is unique in that it enables anyone with a good idea to be successful if they Think Big. One of the greatest impediments to thinking big is a reluctance to work hard. Most of us have seen how the rich live. Shows such as "Lifestyles of the Rich and Famous" get people fantasizing about opulent lifestyles. What is not shown is the hard work that had to precede the wealth. Thinking big means acting big, working hard, and achieving dreams. It absolutely requires courage and commitment. Strap on your gear, if you're ready. Climb the mountain; don't sit around waiting for a helicopter to take you to the top.

7

PRINCIPLE 5

Build Relationships

Human relationships always help us to carry on because they always presuppose further developments, a future—and also because we live as if our only task was precisely to have relationships with other people.

ALBERT CAMUS

I admire Warren Buffett, CEO of Berkshire-Hathaway, and how he invests in people. He is a genius who from modest beginnings has grown his company into a multibillion dollar giant. Buffett spends a lot of time with the key leaders in companies he is considering as candidates for making investments. He observes them, listens to them, and sees firsthand how they treat their colleagues, subordinates, suppliers, and customers. Buffett asks three crucial questions: "Do I like them?" "Do I trust them?" and "Do I respect them?"

A no on any of the big three questions and there is no Berkshire-Hathaway investment or further interest. Buffett cares about how good the financials look and about the investment's market growth potential. How-

145

ever, it is the three relationship questions that first must come back yes, yes, yes. Joining up and forming relationships with people he does not like, trust, and respect means "no" deal for Buffett. I agree with him 100 percent.

The only modification I make to Mr. Buffett's approach in my own analysis of people is asking whether the person is positive. I might like, trust, and respect someone, but if he or she is a negative person, a complainer, a whiner, I move away as fast as possible. Here is my add-on question to Mr. Buffett's "big three": "Is the person positive?" I look for yes answers on Mr. Buffett's three questions and my fourth question. Four yes answers and maybe a relationship should be started.

Avoid at All Costs

I avoid relationships with cynical, can't-do, unethical people. I don't want to spend even one minute with this kind of person.

Every day I come in contact with so many great people. Occasionally, a bad person crosses my path, and I use my experience and gut reaction to move away quickly.

A complainer, whiner, or generally negative person saps your energy. He or she is a taker. I want to be a giver and to work with other givers. In interviewing candidates for Gallery positions, I work at attempting to determine if the interviewee is a taker or giver. I'll ask what in their last job they enjoyed the most and disliked the most. The responses often reveal whether the person gives or takes more. The givers' discussions of what they disliked are muted, while the takers' discussions go on and on, in depth, about a lousy policy, an ignorant coworker, a horrible pay system or schedule. My approach is not scientific, but it is revealing and informative. It helps me make a selection decision.

MACK'S GUIDE TO FINDING HELPERS

People want to help me. My charming personality is not the reason. Charm is not a part of my makeup. Yet, in looking at my career, my family, and my deep relationships, I believe that I actually have a few redeeming characteristics that attract people. Everyone needs helpers to be successful in business and life. You can win helpers to your cause by developing the following characteristics.

Be Optimistic

You need to work at being the opposite of the can't-do person. Get out of bed optimistic each day. Smile, help others, and work hard. Loafing, wasting time, and coasting can kill optimism. Keep these behaviors at a distance.

At Gallery we have the best employees in the industry. No one can beat their energy, work ethic, their enthusiasm in going the extra mile, and their ability to listen and respond to customers. They are exceptional and help each other to maintain their delight-the-customer spirit.

Don't underestimate the power of optimism. It works in business and at home. Enthusiasm and optimism result in providing the steady message to Gallery employees: "They make the difference." Without enthusiastic employees, Gallery would be just another large furniture store with a gigantic warehouse full of furniture waiting to be delivered late. By being optimistic, you attract others to you. A smile is infectious. It can lighten up a room, an office, a meeting.

Ask for Help

Don't be afraid to ask for help. When I need something, such as advice, a critique of a sales plan, a pool of new job candidates, a change in my advertising approach, I ask for help. I pick up the telephone or I make a visit. I can't understand why some people hesitate to ask for help.

People within your circle of friends and colleagues need to know you believe they can help. Waiting until the problem becomes major makes little sense. Don't be afraid to admit you lack the talent, expertise, or answers to solve every problem. Asking for help acknowledges your respect for the person's knowledge or talent.

Be Yourself

Always be natural and free of play acting. Too many people attempt to act like someone else when working with others, often attempting to hold back their ideas, personality, and even speech patterns. They attempt to use their position or a title to get their way. Not being yourself turns people off very quickly. Acting is great in Hollywood. In the work environment it marks you as a phony. It is unattractive, lessens credibility, and creates a wedge between people.

Talk, listen, yell, argue, debate, review, observe, and interact in your natural way. Without acting, you never have to pause and think about how you're doing. Whether in the company of CEOs, a UPS delivery person, mayors of cities, ex-Presidents of the United States, retail clerks, governors, movie stars, your child's teachers, sports celebrities, or world-renowned medical surgeons, be yourself. People are more comfortable with the real person, not some version made up to fit a situation.

Develop Others

Coaching and helping people achieve their goals is very rewarding. For me, finding a person who has never sold furniture and helping him or her become successful is especially fulfilling. Observing this person grow on the job as a salesperson is also very gratifying. Educating others so that they have successful careers is a very fulfilling endeavor.

It takes different amounts of time to develop people. I had to learn this over the years. I wouldn't accept
the individual-difference logic and thought that everyone should be a super salesperson in about one year,
even if the person had no previous sales experience.
My expectations were off base. I was just plain wrong.
People grow, learn, and mature in their jobs at different
rates. My lack of patience resulted in intervening too
forcefully when someone wasn't growing at my preconceived correct rate. There is no right development
rate or maturing cycle. People have different patterns
of learning and developing the skills needed to do their
jobs. Be patient and be aware of differences. It is these
differences that make work interesting, challenging,
and give us broader perspective.

By adjusting your thinking, reigning in impatience,
and observing progress at different rates, you can learn
how to be more of a leader. Developing a respect and
appreciation of individual differences usually takes
some work. The work is worth it, especially when you
begin to witness the development process. By following these guidelines, my own authoritarian approach
gave way to a more sensitive style that respected individual differences. I learned that Gallery employees
are different from one another—and from me. Thank-
fully, these differences make leading others interesting.

Share the Rewards

My success at Gallery is the result of having great people as employees. I know this sounds trite, but it's true. I set the course, and my people execute the details. I referee, motivate, explain where we are going, and do all the advertising. The Gallery team does everything else. Thus, any rewards Gallery receives must be shared. It isn't difficult to know that people who are recognized, praised, and financially rewarded feel appreciated.

Every quarter I call everyone together at Gallery to explain the financial results, share our successes, and provide reward and bonus information. I tell it exactly like it is in reality. My people learn exactly how much revenue we produced for the quarter and what our costs and net profits were. I am an open book for the Gallery team. Each member knows exactly what the revenues, costs, and profits are, how much is available for bonuses, and where improvements can be implemented.

It is important for me to stand in front of everyone during this quarterly meeting and thank them for their contributions. We have fun by sharing stories of delighting customers. I also ask eight or ten people to stand up and tell how they provided extraordinary service to delight a customer. Good examples and stories are contagious and educational. Everyone learns something, and this is rewarding.

Helpers Are Important

If you do your own honest self-inventory, you'll find the people around you help make you a success. Once you accept this fact, surround yourself with talented people with whom you'll gladly share credit for success. There is still a myth that a lot of people believe in regarding the lone genius. However, as we all know, Nobel Prize winners, Pulitzer Prize winners, great surgeons—the Pope himself—and great athletes all have people who contribute to their success. Even the great artist Picasso worked side-by-side with contributors in developing great art. Unless you are a hermit in a mountain hideaway, your ability to survive and prosper will depend to a great extent on the bonds and alliances you form with people.

To find great helpers, you have to be optimistic, be willing to ask for help, be yourself, develop their skills, and share the rewards.

RELATIONSHIP PLANNING

Referring to anything as relationship planning is fairly stiff and impersonal. I want, however, to let you know that building relationships requires a plan. It isn't simple because a plan requires that time, energy, and effort go into charting a course. Plans point the way, steer, and remind you of needed changes. My planning program works wonders for my approach to building relationships. It helps set the tone and points out areas that must be addressed. I work to pay attention and refer to each of these six areas in bolstering and improving my relationships:

1. Listen to Your Special Team
2. Find a Mentor
3. Get to the Person's Core
4. Diversify Your Team
5. Personalize Relationships
6. Be Patient

LISTEN TO YOUR SPECIAL TEAM

I believe in the 80/20 rule in relationships; that is, a handful of acquaintances, friends, and family members are responsible for 80 percent of your relationship time, learning, and development. My 80-percent group includes Linda, my father George, Gallery work colleagues, my sister Mary, and my advertising and public relations guru, Brenda. Asking these individuals for advice and using them as sounding boards for ideas is now a habit. They tell me what I don't want to hear more often than I thought was possible.

Each category of my special team, my "board of directors," has met my own special tests for inclusion. The "Mack Team" includes strong, confident people who listen. Listening is a forgotten trait most people take for granted. Linda listens, processes the words and ideas, and, in no holds barred fashion, responds. She is first a listener.

For example, I wanted to bring back a college football bowl game to Houston. For years Houston hosted the Bluebonnet Bowl which ended because of poor attendance and dwindling revenues. Why would a furniture store owner want to bring a previously faded, end-of-the-season football bowl to Houston? To me, sports advertising and marketing is a powerful promotion tool. I kept talking about promoting Gallery through a new bowl game to Linda. She listened, asked question after question, and didn't embrace the idea for some time. What Linda became for a long while was an honest sounding board. She didn't patronize me, but she did challenge me.

Take your time, use the 80/20 rule, and build your own board of directors. Find the one board member who serves as your chairperson. Linda is mine. The chairperson has to be honest, a good listener, and unafraid to tell you to shape up and do the right thing. A chairperson is the centerpiece of my relationship planning and style.

FIND A MENTOR

Everyone has mentors—special, supportive, and usually older people who teach them the ropes to know and the ropes to skip. I am an unashamed proponent of Dr. W. Edwards Deming's approach—total quality management approach (TQM). When he was alive, he was on my special team. He was also my adopted mentor, though I adopted him without telling

him he was mentoring me. Gallery was thriving during Houston's boom years in the early 1980s. Customers, sales, profits, and brand identity were all coming
together nicely. However, when the economy turned
sour in the late 1980s, I knew changes would have to
be made. I was going to have to help Gallery reinvent
itself from the inside out. Total quality management
seemed to be a good starting point.

I studied total quality management by reading, listening to tapes, and watching videos. Then, I decided
to continue by attending a Crosby quality seminar in
Florida. I listened to what Philip Crosby trainers told
the audience and me. Mr. Crosby wrote a best-selling
book called *Quality Is Free.* The book and the seminar
emphasized that quality is conformance to require-
ments.

My sister, Mary, also went to a Crosby seminar to
hear just what was being taught. Like Linda, she is
honest, listens well, and is very smart. She liked some,
but not all, of what she heard. Mary, however, was
honest and told me that what Gallery was doing had
to be fixed, and the Crosby emphasis on quality was a
good starting point. After the Crosby seminar experience, to improve quality, Gallery started to emphasize
preventing a problem rather than fixing it.

Still, I was a little skeptical about one Crosby concept that states that "perfect performance equals zero
defects." Who can always be perfect? As long as people are involved, perfection is going to be more of an
unattainable goal than a reality. The concept of perfec-

tion just didn't seem reasonable when dealing with such people as employees, customers, or family members. Personally, I know how imperfect I am and felt that thinking in terms of perfection would lead to too much disappointment, dishonesty, and avoidance.

After starting with the Crosby approach, a friend told me about Dr. Deming. I watched a few of Dr. Deming's videos and decided to attend one of his seminars. He had helped the Japanese rebuild their entire industrial infrastructure after World War II. In the 1950s, Japanese products were considered worthless in the world markets. Dr. Deming introduced the Japanese to his concepts of total quality management, statistical quality control, and cooperation that started the Japanese on the road to economic recovery and rebuilding.

I was impressed with Dr. Deming as a person, teacher, and statistician. I was so impressed that I attended seminar after seminar. I believe I attended ten of his four-day workshops. He listened and responded to my endless stream of questions. He was adamant about not using incentive pay systems. I was having big trouble at Gallery because of the pay system that was creating cutthroat competition among the sales team. They were fighting for customers, arguing about who made which sale, and generally being cranky with everyone.

When I became a repeat and serial attendee of Dr. Deming's seminars, I decided to take along a number of Gallery employees. At one of the seminars I met Carl Seville, a very successful Dallas car dealer. During the seminar breaks we talked business. He told me that he eliminated his commissioned sales pay plan, and the results had been happier sales personnel, more sales, and more cooperation, exactly the results Dr. Deming was telling us about again and again.

I kept attending seminars, talked to Dr. Deming about Gallery eliminating commissioned sales pay, and heard his response to do away with it now. I asked him again and heard the same response. Commissioned pay leads to cutthroat competition among a sales team. Gallery had already abolished performance appraisals after Dr. Deming illustrated and convinced me that they can damage enthusiasm, commitment, and even loyalty. Though we really never used a full-blown formal appraisal system at Gallery, we did experiment with some rather loose systems. At Gallery, when we used appraisals, they were only report cards and personality beauty contests. We just wanted to stop giving adult employees report cards. It is better to observe every day. A better approach is to talk, listen, walk around, and watch your employees every single day. Gallery is in the customer-delight not the rates-you business! Abolishing appraisal systems was easy because we never liked them to start with and they are so negatively tilted.

I continue to recall, reread, and think hard about the teachings, lessons, and philosophy of Dr. Deming. I have used his system of profound knowledge to build and sustain relationships. He always discussed the transformation of a person, and his message and teachings transformed me. Dr. Deming taught that once a person is transformed, he or she will be influential.

Borrowing from My Mentor, Dr. Deming

- *Set an example.*
- *Be a good listener but do not compromise.*
- *Continually teach other people.*
- *Help other people pull away from their current practices and beliefs and move into the new philosophy without feeling guilty about the past.*

I combined Dr. Deming's lessons about transformation with his 14 Points for Management and incorporated them in the entire Gallery operation. The 14 Points have as their goal: Make it possible for people to work with joy. The Deming system as adapted also results in better relationships, more customer-delight opportunities, and improved management practices. These three results have certainly helped Gallery succeed.

Point 10, involving imposing a zero defects target, is always one that captures my interest. At the Dr. Deming Seminars the "Red Bead Experiment" illustrated the problem with going for zero defects. Six volunteers are asked to scoop beads from a box using a trowel. The goal is to scoop only white beads. The box contains 20 percent red and 80 percent white beads.

Scooping with the trowel, the volunteers again and again come up with red beads. No matter how the volunteers scooped, red beads appeared. Dr. Deming praised, barked instructions, and asked for new volunteers with no success. He illustrated very clearly that the system was at fault, not the volunteers. Blaming workers for system problems beyond their control is poor leadership and damages any relationship between the leader and the other persons.

Dr. Deming taught me that Gallery Furniture had to change its system to improve its service to satisfy customers. The relationship between Gallery and its customers, suppliers, employees, and the community could only be changed by transforming the system. Planning such a transformation took patience, knowledge, a willingness to take some risks, and the monitoring of progress or lack of progress.

Just as Dr. Deming became my mentor, you need your own special mentor, someone you respect and are open with in expressing thoughts, dreams, and plans. Being completely open is very difficult. A clergyman, friend, relative, teacher, or work colleague can provide the mentor guidance needed. It's up to you to build mentor relationships with people, even if you have to adopt them without their knowing, as I did.

GET TO THE PERSON'S CORE

Before taking a relationship seriously and using it to create a win-win scenario, it is important to determine the other person's agenda. What does the other person want to achieve? You have to listen for and observe what the person has in mind. If the person's agenda is to make as much money as possible no matter what, you have to determine whether this fits your agenda. Sharing an agenda, values, needs, dreams, and interest is a must in any relationship planning and building. Search for people who have the core values that are important to you. At Gallery, we want to delight customers and give back to others; nothing complicated, just a plain, focused agenda. I focus on finding others with these core values.

MACK CASE

Faith in People Results in Strong Relationships

One of my models of how to build relationships with employees and community is Aaron Feurestein, CEO of Malden Mills in Lawrence, Massachusetts. A few years ago a devastating fire swept through his factory, threatening the closing of the plant and the loss of over 2,000 jobs. Mr. Feurestein promised his employees that their jobs were secure. He focused on rebuilding Malden Mills and continued to provide paychecks and benefits during the rebuilding.

What a wonderful example of a leader with faith in his people. Mr. Feurestein is a great role model for any business leader.

An employee, a job candidate, a supplier of furniture needs to show me that customer satisfaction and generosity are on the top of their lists. It's critical for me to have relationships with people I believe in because then I am confident that together we can accomplish what is important to us. If you build relationships with people whose goals and values are like yours, you will have true partners.

Trust is vital to any relationship, and trust building starts when you have partners who share your goals, dreams, values, and agenda. You don't have to spend a lot of time building a relationship if trust is there to start the process. Remember what we said in Chapter 3, "Promises made, promises kept." If you want to build trust, start with keeping your promises.

DIVERSIFY YOUR TEAM

You have to build a diverse team. The notion of a special mentor implies diversity. A mentor is probably going to be older and more experienced. By having a special mentor you are beginning to diversify. You are probably going to have to work hard at fighting off building a "just like me" relationship team. We are in the business of selling furniture and delighting customers of every possible background. Our customer base is young, old, Hispanic, Asian, White, and African-American. It's these customers who have helped Gallery succeed. I have relationships with people who are not like me because I want to diversify and grow professionally and personally.

Limiting yourself to relationships with people who see the world in the same way you do limits your perspective. It stunts your growth. Always surrounding yourself with people just like you may be comfortable in the short run, but it will be disastrous in the long run. You narrow your view of the world. You use a telescope, but you need something with a broader lens.

Spending Time with Others

I try to find an opinion the opposite of mine when I want a different view about a business problem. Forming relationships with people who are not like me is important because it results in many kinds of answers, suggestions, and ideas.

Invest your time in developing relationships with people who don't always look like you, are of different ages, and come from different backgrounds. You can do this better by taking time to listen, learn, share, trust, and exchange ideas about values. Act naturally, and people from every background possible will want to help you.

When Gallery opened its doors and for a number of years after, we searched for employees who resembled Linda and me: High-energy, self-starting, fast-talking, and independent. Gallery ended up with a lot of people who could care less about customer loyalty, hated their jobs, and were undependable. We tried to take a few characteristics that fit Linda and me and use them to model my team. Wrong approach!

We found that customers were such a diverse group that a one-size salesperson didn't fit everyone. Some customers wanted and needed a Spanish-speaking salesperson. Other customers wanted a middle-aged, experienced-looking salesperson to help them plan their living room arrangement. A diverse team became a must for doing business. Experience helped us see the light, and Gallery worked hard at building a young, old, male, female, African-American, White, Asian, and Hispanic relationship team.

By having a diverse relationship team, Gallery is able to make better business decisions and find ways to delight customers in a lot of different ways. For example, Gallery has a 265,000 square foot showroom. Getting around is a chore even for the young, nimble customers. Older customers needed some help moving around the store. A number of Gallery employees, the older ones, suggested purchasing golf type scooters for the older folks. Eureka! The scooters are a big hit and help the older customers get from one end of the showroom to the other.

MACK LESSON

Celebrate Diversity

The diverse Gallery team brings into meetings ideas for music in the store, foods to serve, colors of fabrics, financing plans, and a literally limitless stream of assorted suggestions. Gallery couldn't be suc-

cessful without the ability to tune into the different ages, ethnicity, income levels, languages, customs, and culture of its customers. We are in the business of delighting customers who come from around-the-world backgrounds. This is part of the reason that Gallery is truly the world's furniture store.

PERSONALIZE RELATIONSHIPS

In a lifetime you learn that personalizing relationships is hard but necessary work. You have to make it clear to people that your relationship with them is important. Know the people, their families, and their backgrounds. Do whatever it takes to personalize. For example, if you know a person's nickname, place of birth, or favorite sports team, use this information to personalize the relationship. As a test, stop now and make a list of the ten people you value the most and try to list five personal tidbits on each person. How did you do? If you can't personalize, you're not using relationships effectively.

A critical part of personalization is being honest. Don't try to fake it. If you fake, it will be obvious. If the relationship is a must, then you have to do your homework and really learn something about the person. This starts with listening carefully to what the person says. In the furniture business, I talk every day with people. I don't always listen carefully, but I am getting better with age. I try to be so focused on the person I am talking or listening to that sometimes I scare them off with my intensity.

After most of my 300 annual speeches, there is usually a question and answer session. Listening is a part of the process. This listening experience helps me in building my relationships. By listening to audiences, I have become better at listening to colleagues at Gallery and to other people in my network of acquaintances and friends. You will learn that everyone wants to be treated as the main attraction, a movie star.

MACK LESSON

Treat Everyone Like a Movie Star

You must focus on the person you are talking or listening to so they feel special. Stop looking around, stretching, checking your watch. Each of these is a signal that the other person is not important. The other person can tell when and if you are giving them short shrift. Make eye contact, ask questions, use their name, nod, and smile to personalize the interaction.

You must refine your approach to listening to others. Always listen intently. By listening intently, you are able to really learn about the other person. A person talking to you is communicating through their stories, language, pauses, body language, hand movements, and unique inflections. People easily pick up your signals of listening intently.

BE PATIENT

Relationship planning and building take time. Even though there is no set limit for building a relationship, be sure to allow enough time. To build trust in other people and have them feel comfortable around you, you are going to have to observe and listen to them over a period of time. Thus, relationship building requires patience.

Yet, a lot of people, myself included, are not very patient. Building trusting relationships requires time and patience. Learn to set aside time, slowly increasing your patience range.

The trust element in a relationship is the glue that holds it together through ups and downs. At Gallery, I have learned I must trust some people besides Linda. If you can't trust, you will not be able to delegate or allow people to make their own decisions. The patience and time required to build trust are worth the effort. Trust is built up when a customer, colleague, or supplier feels that you have taken the time to make them feel important, as important as a movie star.

Some businesses monitor their employees at work. Listening to telephone calls, cameras in work areas, and time cards for punching in and out are all monitoring tools. Monitoring is established because of distrust. Sometimes an employee proves to be untrustworthy. There are a few bad apples in every barrel. But a few bad employees should not force you to install a big-brother system to catch employees loafing, stealing, or treating a customer badly. I will never resort to a monitoring system at Gallery Furniture. My relationships with Gallery employees are built on a solid foundation of trust.

These six steps form the core of a relationship planning approach. Each one is important: Building a special team, having a special mentor such as the late Dr. W. Edwards Deming, learning about the core values of potential relationship partners, diversifying your relationship network, personalizing the relationship by practicing intense listening, and being patient to build trust. Like playing a musical instrument, you have to work hard, starting with planning. Your goal should be to get better at relationship planning and building.

Being successful in business relationships means being ethical, fair, open, and concerned about the other person. Also, support your family by giving them time and patience. Building community relationships means helping others, volunteering, and keeping your promises. You'll find that by building better relationships, more people will want to help you succeed.

8

PRINCIPLE 6

Always Think Big

A ship in port is safe, but that's not what ships are built for.

GRACE MURRAY HOPPER

No long-term personal or business benefits come from thinking small. People who think small spend a lot of time wondering, "What if?" That's tragic. Most people don't Think Big because doing so involves taking risks. Thinking Big means stepping outside of your comfort zone and trying new things. Going outside of your comfort zone means putting stress on yourself.

Everyone has a pain threshold when it comes to the stress they are willing and able to tolerate. Most people approach that threshold from time to time and then pull back. They believe that whatever lies beyond that point must be bad because it feels painful just to get close to that point. They don't understand that business and personal success is derived from pushing that threshold back farther and farther. Remember, most successful people never do make it to some sort of heaven on earth; they still experience stress, pain, and unhappiness. They've learned the valuable lesson that success is relative, and it comes from approaching one's limits, exceeding them, pushing back their tolerance for stress, and then retreating momentarily to recoup, learn, and do it again.

Thinking Big drives people and business systems to their limits. Thinking Big helps people visualize how business will be when they push their limits out just a little farther. Thinking Big helps people realize that pushing their limits further out adds value to their companies. It enables them to do just a little more today than they were able to do yesterday. Thinking Big adds excitement and zest to life. It means that momentary setbacks or frustrations are viewed as challenges, not calamities. People who Think Big believe their destiny lies beyond where they are today. They have a sense of the possible that's more important to them than the actual. Thinking Big means setting and achieving goals. It means being creative and solving problems. It means being optimistic and positive. It means expanding the variety and spice of life.

Thinking Big has had tremendous effects on Gallery Furniture. Thinking Big has more or less always been a part of my nature. When I was a not-too-good football player, I walked on and made the team at the powerhouse University of Texas. When I wasn't satisfied with just a single store, I started a chain of health clubs. When I opened Gallery, I wasn't satisfied with doing business like all the other furniture stores in town. Thinking Big requires a mindset that ignites creativity and powers decision-making and planning. I have boiled this mindset down to the following four key elements:

1. Vision
2. A Sense of Entitlement
3. Action Plans
4. Managing Resources

VISION

Some people sneer at the concept of vision, but it's essential to Thinking Big. You can't reach for the stars if you don't envision yourself traveling on a beam of light. You can't become a big leaguer without spending hours upon hours in your backyard envisioning the crowd, game situations, and glorious victories. Vision makes the unreachable, reachable—if only in our minds. It sows the seeds of the possible amidst the barren plains of the impossible. Thinking Big means creating a vision of what you'd like to achieve and then doing something to bring it about.

Someone once asked me what my vision for Gallery Furniture was. No one had asked that before, and the question took me somewhat by surprise. It only took a second for me to respond, "My vision for Gallery is better, faster, cheaper." Afterward, it struck me that, in fact, that really *is* my vision. I hadn't thought of it in those terms, but we had created the Gallery systems based on that simple vision. The Gallery philosophy of same-day delivery is consistent with that vision. The Gallery pricing structure is consistent with that vision. The Gallery merchandise is consistent with that vision. And the Gallery focus on customer delight is consistent with that vision. I hadn't consciously created a vision statement, but my internal guide about what I wanted Gallery to be had led to the development of all the systems that make Gallery unique in the world.

The point is that a vision doesn't need to be explicit to be powerful. A good vision, one that is capable of guiding your actions and thoughts, may be nothing more than a compelling idea that you have. Most business owners have some sense of where they'd like to go with their business. This "sense" is a vision.

MACK SPEAK

What Are Your Dreams?

What are your dreams? Do they seem unreasonable? Do they seem out of reach? That just shows how powerful and life-changing they can be. What you can dream, what you can imagine, is possible. What you commit your thoughts and efforts toward achieving, toward creating, toward building, toward becoming, will happen.

My experience tells me that a vision doesn't lead to much change unless it promotes action. The Gallery "better, faster, cheaper" vision would mean nothing if we didn't act on it every day. Notice that the "better, faster, cheaper" vision doesn't have much detail. It provides only a sketch; everyone at Gallery has to fill in the details according to their own interpretation. For me, it means getting involved in multiple marketing and promotional activities, building the Gallery brand, and spreading the Gallery message around the world. For Gallery's buyers, it means going to the best furniture shows in the world and picking out interesting pieces that will meet the ever-changing needs of our customers. For Gallery's designers, it means creating a store environment that becomes a destination for casual weekday and weekend shoppers. For Gallery's salespeople, it means learning how to listen to customers to satisfy their needs and to provide ever-higher levels of service. For Gallery's warehouse people, it means streamlining processes and working in teams to speed up delivery times and minimize errors.

MACK SPEAK

Think Big about Everything

When I'm involved in a promotional event, I always Think Big. I don't want to spend time on projects that aren't going to make a massive difference for Gallery.

Let me give you an example of how I Think Big when building the Gallery brand. A few years ago, I was contacted about sponsoring a college football bowl game. The promoters actually contacted me about 14 months prior to the event. That may seem like a lot of time, but there is an enormous amount of planning that goes into a successful bowl game. You have to make preparations to entertain two teams of football players, each of which comprises some 100 people when you include coaches, trainers, and other support staff. You have to make arrangements to entertain thousands of fans who will be following their teams to the game. You have to make accommodations for the press, television crews, and other media. You have to arrange for ticket sales, marketing, and public relations. All of these things must come together correctly to have a successful bowl experience. The people that approached me to sponsor the GalleryFurniture.com bowl game, mentioned in Chapter 5, wanted to start small and quietly the first year so we could work out the kinks and then grow the event annually.

Early on, I had a lot of clashes with the promoters because my vision of what the bowl game would become was larger than theirs. Their vision was limited to creating an event that appealed to fans of the teams selected for the bowl game. I believed we could generate the fan-based ticket sales, but I also believed we could generate a lot of local interest. Houston had not had a bowl game since the demise of the Astro-Bluebonnet Bowl in the mid-1980s. The Houston Astrodome is still a major sports venue, and I believed we could attract local football fans to the event no matter who was playing. My vision was to create enthusiasm, market like crazy, and tap into local pride about host-ing a major bowl game again.

Eventually, I was able to sell this vision to the promoters. From there, we set out to create a market-ing campaign that would draw crowds regardless of which teams ended up being selected to play. Of course, we hoped that a local team would be invited, but we didn't want to depend on that happening. All of our marketing efforts sought to get people interested in the conferences that would be represented in the bowl. So, it didn't matter who played in the game be-cause people would know that the teams were from a major conference and had played a quality college football schedule to get there. From the original vision of a modest bowl game with mostly team-loyal fans, we transformed it into an event that drew interest from the entire region. We created pregame activities. We crafted promotional events to generate local interest. We made up thousands of t-shirts and other give-aways to develop a perception of growing excitement.

Was the game a success? Absolutely. We did every-thing we said we would to promote the event, take care of the football teams, and provide entertainment for the fans. In the end, we didn't draw as many people to the game as we would have liked, but that is now a challenge for next year.

The GalleryFurniture.com bowl game lived up to the vision we had created for it. From a simple idea, we had developed an event that was part of the national college football bowl season. The power of our vision pulled us through on many occasions when the going was tough. It gave shape to our actions as we used our limited resources to accomplish goals. It provided us with a sense of satisfaction on game day as the event, which we had previously seen only in our mind's eye, unfolded before us on the Astrodome turf. Most importantly, the game carried the Gallery Furniture brand into millions of homes both regionally and nationally. Thinking Big about the Gallery brand now places it alongside such well-known brands as Outback, FedEx, Nokia, and other larger bowl sponsors. Not bad for a single-site furniture store to be listed along with these respected brands.

MACK SPEAK

The Satisfaction of Dreams Realized

I will never tire of the feeling that I get when I've worked long and hard to turn a vision into reality. Happily, I get that feeling nearly every day as I walk the floor of Gallery Furniture and see delighted customers chatting and smiling with our staff because they have just made a purchase that fulfilled their vision.

A SENSE OF ENTITLEMENT

To Think Big you have to believe that you are entitled to Succeed Big. A lot of people don't Think Big because they have a belief that doing so is bad or evil. They believe that they will be punished by society,

God, the universe, or something else if they strive to achieve their dreams. These beliefs are based in part on real world events. Humans have a morbid fascination with seeing the mighty fall. We have an innate fondness for the underdog. We cheer for the little guy against the big guy. When the U.S. Justice Department won a landmark antitrust ruling against Microsoft, the federal prosecutors were actually high-fiving each other on national television. Personally, I found the display disgusting. Though no one approves of monopolies acting in restraint of trade, why should government employees be rejoicing on TV about breaking up the most successful company in history? I'll tell you why. Because they are like everyone else in taking joy at bringing down the mighty.

In order to Think Big, you have to overcome this human tendency to believe that being big means being bad. You have to develop a sense that you and your company are entitled to grow and become great. The U.S. Army used to advertise with the slogan, "Be All You Can Be." The idea was that the Army would provide recruits with the tools they needed to be successful in military battle as well as in the battles of life. I like the whole idea of "being all you can be." To develop a mindset that will allow you to Think Big without feeling guilty, there are three things you can do.

1. *Believe in the human spirit.* When you think about it, the human spirit has virtually no boundaries. Humans used to be confined to small tri-

bal bands but broke beyond that. They used to be confined to walled cities but broke beyond that. They used to be confined to nation states but broke beyond that. They also used to be confined to this planet but are breaking beyond that. The human spirit knows no true boundaries. You have a whisper of that boundless spirit within you—everyone does. You have to believe that you can contribute and expand and allow that spirit to express itself through your actions and deeds.

2. *Learn how systems work.* The world is a complicated place. Many things are beyond your control. Thinking Big means understanding some things about how systems work and how to design systems to achieve goals. In order to become wealthy in business, for example, you must know a little about how business works. Thinking Big means being open to learning at all times. Many managers think they have to know everything because they're afraid to appear less intelligent than their subordinates. I have never had that problem. I surround myself with bright, energetic people. Managers are like symphony conductors. They can't play all the instruments; they just make sure the musicians all play the right notes at the right time.

3. *Be innovative.* Innovation is one of the most important aspects of our success at Gallery. Our sense of entitlement requires that we be

exceedingly resourceful. Anyone in business knows that each business day brings challenges and surprises. Having a culture of innovation enables novel responses to meet head on each challenge and surprise. Gallery employees are encouraged to be creative and innovative to meet our business goals. I'm convinced that our culture of innovation has dramatically increased sales and reduced costs—a manager's dream recipe for success.

I'll give you an example of how these three lessons have been applied at Gallery. We are constantly fighting off competition. Many entrepreneurs who think they have identified the Gallery formula for success open up shop next door or right down the road. On the surface, they try to be as Gallery-like as possible. Some even use tents pitched in the parking lot as retail space. We outsell them every time. We Think Big and welcome competitors. Competition makes us sharper and gives us incentive to work harder than we already do. But we don't feel guilty when the other stores go out of business. That's the nature of a free market. Right? Our economy is a profit-and-loss system. When someone goes out of business, people lose their jobs. We don't feel guilty about this. In fact, we turn and hire the good people who want to work with a winner. We're entitled to be the better competitor.

The challenge I have as a manager at Gallery is to keep the excitement and enthusiasm alive despite our already tremendous achievements. We have the most productive retail store in the world. How do you top that? Our performance continues to astound experts. When they think we can't possibly turn more inventory, we show them that we can. I have learned that believing we can continue to grow is self-fulfilling. As long as we stay focused on our goals and values, we will always find ways to increase sales and reduce our costs.

I am always thinking of ways to leverage current events in a BIG way. When America was attacked on September 11, Gallery responded by flying the biggest American flag in the state. We also gave away t-shirts with the American flag emblazoned on them to everyone who came into Gallery—whether or not they bought anything from us. Gallery is a good neighbor, and we constantly look for ways to convert popular movements into new business. Our belief that we are entitled to enjoy success enables us to leverage every opportunity that comes our way. When Houston was hit by a terrible flood from a tropical storm in the Spring of 2001, we were the first store to respond. We worked with the Federal Emergency Management Agency (FEMA) to ensure that individuals could easily redeem vouchers to replace furniture, mattresses, and electronics destroyed by the flood. We turned a tragedy into a business opportunity because that's what Gallery is entitled to do. Sure we give merchandise to needy families sometimes, but when government money pours in to help distressed families, as a business we are entitled to some of that money if we are responsive and don't take unfair advantage. Did we profit? Sure, but we actually dropped our prices to levels that were barely above cost and gained a whole lot of new, delighted, Gallery customers.

MACK LESSON

A Few Select Rules

If you believe in the human spirit, dedicate yourself to constant learning, and get rid of guilt you will have cleared the way to Thinking Big. By following these rules, you will have cleared the blockages in your mind that prevent 99 percent of people from achieving their dreams. Believe in the human spirit, learn how to express it through your gifts and skills, don't let guilt block your actions, and you will pave the way to Thinking Big.

ACTION PLANS

Although you will need a plan to realize your vision, Thinking Big should occasionally be done with no thoughts at all about what can, in reality, be achieved. Thinking Big requires that you allow yourself and your work team to dream about what you'd like to create for your business.

At Gallery, I sit down regularly with our designers and dream about how we'd like to create a better atmosphere for Gallery's customers. We don't let anything constrain us when we brainstorm for ideas. How else could we have come up with the idea to combine a bowling alley with Elvis's car, Princess Diana's jewelry, and Shaquille O'Neal's size 18 shoes? We Think Big without constraints. We dream, and then we challenge the dream with reality.

When we have our brainstorming sessions at Gallery, all constraints are temporarily ignored so that we can come up with the biggest ideas possible. After that, we choose those ideas we think are the best and develop a plan to achieve them. For example, when I wanted to purchase Elvis's vintage Ford Thunderbird I was unable to get to the auction in Las Vegas where the car was being sold. To realize my vision of owning that car, we planned how to enable me to participate in the bidding process without my actually being there.

One of my assistants went to the event armed with a cell phone. She called me with the latest bid, I replied with my bid, and she made the bid on the auction floor. Of course, all plans have some snags. In the middle of intense bidding, the cell phone died because of interference in the building. Undaunted, my assistant got the latest bid, ran out the front door to call me, and ran back in with my counter bid. In the end, we got the car.

Thinking Big means creating a plan of action to achieve your goals. It means being patient, perseverant, and disciplined. Very few of us will be fortunate enough to win the lottery. That's a good thing because they say that we have less chance of winning the lottery than being struck by lightning, and I don't want to be struck by lightning.

Thinking Big means taking advantage of luck but not relying on it. Everyone needs luck, and usually everyone enjoys a little luck in life. But you can't control when your luck will be good. You can control your actions and the discipline of sticking to an action plan. It's very rare that life and work go exactly as we'd like them to. Being disciplined to see plans through to completion is essential in Thinking Big. All large achievements take time, usually more time than you think.

I've told you that Gallery doesn't have a formal business plan. I'm a bit unconventional in that regard, and I certainly don't suggest that business plans aren't necessary to good business. Gallery doesn't have a business plan because we have a simple, clear set of values that guide us and an easy way to measure success. Literally, we measure success by our bank account. Gallery doesn't buy anything on credit. When I look into the Gallery bank account, I know exactly what we have and how much we have made since the last time I looked.

With that simple approach, I've never felt the need for a business plan, although we do a lot of action planning. We use simple systems that allow our people to focus on customers. For example, same-day delivery means we can only sell items that we have in our warehouse. We need a system that helps us keep track of the unit sales of each item so that we can keep our promise of same-day delivery. Our system is as simple as you can imagine. We count the number of units in the warehouse and keep the same number of tickets for each item at the point of sale. Each time we sell a unit, we remove a ticket. When the tickets are gone, the warehouse is empty. Simple.

Good Luck Can Be Cultivated

There are things in life over which you have control, and there are things over which you have little or no control. Both contribute to luck. Through positive focus, discipline, preparation, effort, and persistence anyone can get lucky. I have always believed that good luck will be yours if you work your way toward it.

Our action plans at Gallery always include tasks and names of people assigned to the tasks. They also include projected time frames for completion. We are able to judge our progress by how well we are doing in regard to our plans. Of course, all achievement requires that resources be used. Creatively acquiring and then effectively applying resources is the final lesson in Thinking Big.

RESOURCES

Back in the early days, Gallery was operated with extremely limited resources. During that time, Linda and I spent many hours of each day thinking of ways to make it to the next day. We had limited resources of people, time, and cash. Each business goes through this phase at some time. Thinking Big means believing that you will find the resources you need when you need them to achieve your goals. A famous football coach once said, "We didn't lose, we just ran out of time." That saying applies to business as well. Businesses that go bankrupt don't lose, they just run out of ideas to find new resources or to stretch existing ones.

One of the lessons that I learned at Gallery is that most businesses have more resources than they realize. In general, we're a wasteful society that believes most things are disposable. Well, it's amazing how things that we thought were useless can be converted into a valuable resource. I'll give you an example.

In the early days, Gallery had a lot more furniture than we had space for in the showroom. More than half of our furniture was actually displayed in the parking lot exposed to whatever the elements would throw at it. Many times my staff and I had to race around with plastic sheets to cover furniture when a sudden thunderstorm broke out. It didn't take long for me to realize that we had to protect that furniture better. I looked around for some ideas and found a company that rented and erected tents for picnics and other outdoor events. They had some old tents that they were going to throw out. I asked if I could buy them, and they readily agreed to let me have them very cheap.

Now, these weren't ordinary tents. These were very large tents that had massive support poles, yards of canvas, and cartons full of ropes, stakes, and flaps. We took the tents back to Gallery and put them up in the parking lot. When we moved the furniture under the tents we found that this strategy was a hit. People loved to shop under the tents, and, what's more, our furniture was now protected from the elements. We used those tents for many years. To this day, Gallery uses tents as showrooms for some of its furniture. Of course, we've upgraded over the years. The tents now have wooden sides, windows, and air conditioning. But back then there was no cheaper retail space on this planet than the space we created under those tents. That was a resourceful decision that we made that helped us immensely in the early days.

Thinking Big means never being concerned that you will be able to obtain the resources you need to achieve your dreams. People who Think Big have an ability not only to get the most out of the limited resources they have, they are also very good at recognizing and gathering resources others might miss. For example, I'll bet a lot of the people who read this book will admit that they've had cash flow problems at some time. Cash flow problems arise because there is a temporary imbalance between the money going out and the money coming in. Everyone experiences this— whether in home finances or in business. Cash is a resource. If you Think Big, you'll realize that there will be times when you have to be creative in how you manage cash. This may require that, from time to time, you reach out to creditors and ask for more time to make a payment. Business owners do this all the time. In a cash flow crunch, they identify their creditors and try to figure out which ones need to be paid immediately and which ones can be put off. It's amazing how lenient some creditors will be if they are informed about your cash problems. Most are interested in helping you because they want their money back at some point.

A popular book, titled *Rich Dad, Poor Dad*, advocates that people pay themselves first and their creditors last. This idea has merit, but it can be abused. As long as people don't *overpay* themselves first, the concept is a good one. Remember, creditors are rational. They want to get their money back, but not if it means putting you in a position where they jeopardize future business with you. People who are chronically behind in payments to creditors need to change their spending habits. People who occasionally run into cash flow problems can deal with them by being open with creditors. Thinking Big will inevitably bring you into situations where your cash inflow doesn't match your cash outflow. You need to be able to think creatively in the allocation of your resources so that you don't lose momentum on your path to your goals.

Gallery doesn't worry about cash flow because it doesn't buy anything on credit. Long ago I made a decision that I wanted to have a very simple way of keeping track of how well we're doing. Paying cash for everything means that all I need to do is call the bank to see how much money is in the Gallery account. This gives me tremendous peace of mind. It doesn't mean that we've gotten lazy about maximizing resources, however. We are masters of making something out of nothing. Gallery employees are trained to constantly think of new ways to make the shopping environment better for our customers. We Think Big because we want our customers to brag about the experience they had at Gallery and to tell others to come and see us.

When Gallery hosted the U.S. Men's Clay Court Tennis Championship at the Westside Tennis Club in 2001, we didn't spare any expense in making our customers happy. We had two different sets of customers for this event, players and fans. Some of the Think Big highlights that we arranged for the players included the lounge that we built at the Westside basketball facility—practice home of the Houston Rockets and Houston Comets. We rolled in big-screen TVs, La-Z-Boy loungers, sofas, and other items to give the players a place to feel comfortable and relaxed. We had a continuous buffet of healthy snack foods available, and we made sure that all who had a special diet had foods to meet their needs. We spared no expense in talking to players and their agents to make sure everyone felt that we had done all we could to make them happy. Our efforts must have paid off because, within a few months of the tournament, I ran into the agent for Andre Agassi, and he confirmed that Andre would play in the 2002 tournament.

Taking Care of the Details

We tried to sign up Andre Agassi to a two-year contract, but his agent said, "Look, if he comes to Houston and has a good time, you won't have any problem getting him back." The players at the 2001 tournament were impressed with the attention we paid to details and their comfort. All these guys make a lot of money, but one of the things they liked the most was the fact that we did their laundry for free.

Tennis fans were treated to an equal level of Thinking Big treatment. We made sure that everyone who wanted to get into the matches was able to get in. All tennis tournaments are built around a single-elimination system where players who win a match advance and those who lose no longer play. When there are a lot of players, as in the Men's Clay Court Championship, it takes about a week to play all of the matches and arrive at the championship final. Because casual fans need to know which players are still in the tournament and where and when they are playing, we designed the largest scoreboard ever used at a tennis tournament to keep the fans informed.

It's simple, really. Figure out what people need in order to enjoy their experience and give it to them in a big way. When someone told me that balloons help to make an experience more festive for fans, I got on the phone to my assistant and told her to spare no expense in filling the Westside grounds with balloons.

We had balloons everywhere. People loved it. Kids loved it. And it made the tournament festive and fun for everyone. Did we make money? Yes. Why? Because we practiced Thinking Big and didn't spare any expense in making our customers happy. The more we spend on customers, the more they spend on us. It's a simple relationship that works every time.

FINAL THOUGHTS

This chapter focused on Thinking Big. There's no doubt that Thinking Big is scary for many people. It means visibility, exposure, risk, and uncertainty. It's difficult for most of us to Think Big because it means that we'll be noticed by others. Being noticed means exposing ourselves to potential ridicule and embarrassment. I can't tell you how many times I've been ridiculed. It still happens on a regular basis. But I'll tell you one thing: I don't get embarrassed anymore. Thinking Big has taught me that no good deed goes unpunished. Yes, there will be critics for everything that you do. They will criticize when you fail. They will criticize when you succeed. The only way to avoid critics is to do *nothing* at all.

9

P R I N C I P L E   7

Managing and Marketing Philanthropy

We make a living by what we get, but we make a life by what we give.

W I N S T O N   C H U R C H I L L

One of my great pleasures comes from helping others. Sometimes people believe that successful business owners should have exotic sports cars, homes in every comfortable climate, weekends of entertainment and leisure, expensive jewelry, and private jets. We have been successful at Gallery in delighting customers, which directly leads to selling a lot of furniture. Our success is linked to the community where we are physically located and the city in which we live. Material wealth and its use by me personally are going to have to wait. It is more important for Gallery to give back and to position itself as a solid citizen in the community.

One way of giving back to the community is by creating jobs, writing paychecks, and having a profit-sharing plan for over 300 people. Gallery is not only creating jobs but also wealth. Building a successful furniture business creates wealth that benefits many people. By writing these paychecks, serving customers, and being a good citizen, Gallery is a point of light.

Ex-president George H. Bush talked about a thousand points of light. He was talking about community organizations and people all across America. Helping others who are less fortunate is how we at Gallery can be a point of light. Reaching out, stretching, and touching others with kindness, time, expertise, furniture, and other resources is how we think and act. Good philanthropy equals good business, and that means selling more furniture.

My early history of giving back is not going to win any contest. I did a few things but not enough and usually on a hit-or-miss, sporadic schedule. I observed people helping each other. Gifts of money, food, and clothing are popular. I believe that throughout history Americans have been the most giving people in the world. This kind of giving to others always impressed me, but I was not a regular giving person. I wanted to help, but I often found an excuse to avoid helping out.

Philanthropy's Payoff

Giving to someone else is exciting, especially if you stumbled your-self along the way.

- *Giving to others creates a sense of satisfaction.*
- *Giving back to the community where we live, work, and play makes us feel good.*

Gallery is able to be a centerpiece of giving and charity because of our business success. However, even if we were not a successful business, we could still give time, a helping hand, or special expertise. These are all worthy and are needed in a community. Every community needs many helping hands and minds in addition to jobs and wealth. Without jobs and wealth our community could be like Youngstown, Ohio, Gary, Indiana, and South Chicago, Illinois, where thousands of families languished because the steel mills, foundries, and machine shops closed down in the recession in the early 1980s.

BUILDING COMMUNITY WEALTH

By issuing over 300 paychecks and having a profit-sharing plan for Gallery employees, we are creating wealth. Politicians fascinate me by making claims that they create jobs. Sure, governments create jobs by introducing new programs, agencies, and projects. But it is the business owner who creates wealth by adding jobs.

By delighting customers and holding on to them by keeping our promises, Gallery has grown. This growth has enabled us to hire more people. Delighting customers takes time, patience, and creativity. The process is labor-intensive, and this means hiring more employees. The more we hire, the more wealth we create in the community. We are able to fuel the economy, which raises the standard of living and quality of lives of employees and their families.

MACK LESSON

Watchful Neighbors

The community observes everything and every action done by a business. If you want to earn the community's respect, be a neighbor who cares and treats everyone with respect. It's easy to do if you take the time to be involved in causes that you are passionate about. Your business benefits will far exceed the time, effort, and hard work devoted to those causes.

A COMMUNITY HERO

After denying in my early days that it is hard for one person to make a difference, I have changed my view in the last few years. To understand how one person can make a difference, think about the story of

Candy Lightner. In 1980, her 13-year-old daughter was struck by an erratic, swerving car and died. The driver had a long record of arrests for drunken driving and had been released on bail for hit-and-run driving while under the influence just a few days before. He was drunk again and struck and killed Cari Lightner.

Candy Lightner got angry when a veteran police office told her the perpetrator of the crime probably would not serve any time in jail. Mrs. Lightner tried to see then Governor Jerry Brown for weeks. Finally, he agreed to talk to her and finally told her he would appoint a task force to look into drunk driving.

Candy Lightner had only started. She then organized the group called Mothers Against Drunk Driving (MADD). The movement caught fire and now has over 300 chapters and over 600,000 volunteers and donors.

COMMUNITY INVOLVEMENT

Gallery donates to many different community-related organizations. However, there are a few community giving projects that are especially important. Gallery has selected a few candidates for giving back.

Children are one of the top priorities for everyone at Gallery. Helping them become better citizens and better educated is important. When I started jumping up and down years ago on television with Gallery's "save you money" ads, my face became recognized. I was asked a few times to speak to kids in schools.

After a few rambling speeches, I decided to dedicate my time and energy to giving anti-drug speeches. Drugs are such a problem in society that adults need to pitch in and help kids fight the problem.

Now, I give my anti-drug speeches about four times a week, about 150 times or more a year. In a typical year I talk to over 30,000 kids. As a result, teachers come into Gallery and buy furniture. Now we are also getting young adults whom I talked to at a school 10 or 15 years ago coming into Gallery to purchase furniture. My community giving is a form of indirect promotion of the Gallery brand. This can be called accidental promotion and marketing, accidental because we never imagined the impact on the business of talking to kids in schools, business leaders at luncheons, or participants at national conventions.

The Houston Livestock Show and Rodeo has become a major event in Houston. Youngsters come from all over Texas and the United States to compete for prizes and scholarships. Over 10,000 volunteers, Gallery employees included, orchestrate the Houston Livestock Show and Rodeo.

At the close of the show, usually a Saturday afternoon, an auction for the prize champion steer is held. The money to purchase the prized steer is used for creating scholarships. My first efforts at the auction were unnerving. I planned to buy a nonprize or very common steer for maybe $1,000. This was going to be practice and a just-for-fun purchase. My ego got in the way of my bids, and I found myself bidding $50,000,

$52,000, $65,000. I was caught up in the bidding. My final bid of $97,000 was the winner. I had bid $96,000 above my preset limit. Keep me away from auctions.

The money went to scholarships, which made Gallery happy. The headlines in the paper and the picture showed me with my new friend, a $97,000 steer. The buzz at the Houston Livestock Show and Rodeo was, "Mack paid $97,000 for the grand champion." Again, accidental marketing brought people into the store talking about the steer, the newspaper story, and the charity auction.

Gallery did a good thing for the kids, and quite a number of scholarships were created. What a great feeling. We made a difference. In addition, customers came to the store in droves thanking us for the auction bid. We paid for scholarships, and we accidentally drew customers into the store. I'd call this a big win-win consequence. At the 2001 Rodeo, I bought another grand champion steer, but this time it cost me over $650,000. That's a lot of scholarships.

All business owners have an obligation to give back to the children in their communities. Kids are the future of the country. What is more important? If you give a kid a hand today in the form of a scholarship, a computer, or a weekend or summer job, the payoff is unlimited tomorrow. Who is better positioned to give to kids than successful businesspersons?

The word *obligation* scares a lot of people, but it is appropriate. Who else but successful businesspersons can create jobs, show firsthand how to operate a business, and provide support for education and teachers. After all, businessowners are teachers every single day. It is an important obligation that can benefit businessowners as much as the kids. What a feeling to see the smile on the face of a scholarship winner or the kid you put to work at Gallery. Those smiles are Gallery's thank you for being a point of light in our own small way.

EVERYDAY REQUESTS

Gallery receives hundreds of requests for help each month. The ones that don't interest me involve money schemes. "If you can give me $20,000, I'll pay you back in $5,000 increments when I can." "I want to start a business training canaries to talk." "I need $3,000 to visit a friend in Las Vegas." Requests like these fall on deaf ears.

When kids need something to keep them in school or to find work or when people have had a disastrous fire, Gallery will listen. We don't always say yes. To do so would cost us millions of dollars each month. We are profitable, but Gallery is not the U.S. Mint. Of course, one of our regular donations is furniture or appliances that we have in stock. Imagine how valued a mattress is to a family who has lost all their worldly goods in a devastating fire.

Business owners have to weigh each request for help, support, or goods. Gallery doesn't have a so-phisticated system or method for evaluating general requests. The best I can offer is to hear out the requests and avoid throwing money at everything. In fact, my advice is to not throw money at most requests. Giving back time, scholarships (money indirectly), services and expertise, and goods (furniture and appliances for Gallery) is a more focused way of making a contribution.

THE BIG FLOOD

One June 5, 2001 and June 8, 2001, my community—Houston, Texas—was hit with a devastating, once-in-a-lifetime flood. It started on June 5th when double-digit amounts of rainfall closed a lot of the highways and started to flood housing areas. Then on June 8th tropical storm Allison began to drop 25 inches to 35 inches of rain on parts of Houston in 36 hours. As of December 2001, estimates are that over 3,600 homes were destroyed, 43,000 homes damaged, 22 lives were lost, and there was an estimated $5 billion in property damage, with about $2 billion damage in the world famous Texas Medical Center (11 hospitals, 40,000 employees). Over 90,000 families have filed for federal assistance. The estimates and the devastation are severe even for an area familiar with flooding, hurricanes, and tornados.

There is an old saying that the "worst flood ever" is the one that pours into your home, not the guy's on the news. Only tropical storm Claudette in July 1979 rivals Allison's total rainfall. It dumped over 40 inches of rain in some Houston-area neighborhoods in one day. I wasn't living in Houston in 1979, but I've heard stories about the devastation.

After the flood hit, Houstonians, like Americans everywhere on September 11, 2001, rolled up their sleeves and pitched in to help put the city and region back together. Gallery received hundreds of requests for weeks after June 8, 2001, for money, furniture, and appliances. We teamed up with the Red Cross and the Houston Rockets to provide financial support, and we made special arrangements with Simmons Company to provide money, furniture (especially mattresses), and appliances at deep discounts for flood victims. A lot more needs to be done, and Gallery intends to be a part of the community team leading the recovery.

ACCIDENTAL MARKETING

Through all of the community involvement, Gallery has benefited by creating new customers. Old customers appreciate what we're doing and keep coming back, and our name is mentioned again and again. Any marketing professor will tell you that "branding" is an important promotional concept. *Branding* occurs when a business uses a name, a phrase, a logo, symbols, or combination of these to distinguish itself from competitors. Apple computer puts its logo on its machines and in its ads. Gallery Furniture annually presents thousands of 30-second ads stating that we can "save you money." This is part of our brand.

To communicate with customers, Gallery uses advertising, sales promotions, personal selling, public relations, and philanthropy. The community involvement of Gallery has evolved from accidental marketing into strategic and focused marketing. It is built on our desire, interest, and goal of giving back to kids, people in need, and the community. What started out as the accidental attraction of customers to the store is now a crusade to win the competition battle.

Gallery's approach is to communicate again and again who we are, where we are, and what we have. To us, less is more. Keep the message crisp, simple, and honest. Keep every promise you communicate. The method is to place a massive wave of 30-second commercials on every outlet in the region. Gallery has created a brand by oversimplifying the message.

The formal promotional programs and the community giving programs are "in sync" at Gallery. We keep the promotional message simple, and we give back in many different ways as representatives of Gallery Furniture. My promotional messages are delivered in my best clothes: Khaki pants and a Gallery golf shirt. Everything is simple, including my wardrobe.

ON THE BUSY HIGHWAY

Gallery's physical location is not in the ideal spot or on a tree-shaded lane. It is, however, on one of the busiest highways in the city. People can't miss our signs. We are in sight of thousands of potential customers driving by daily. There are also the thousands of 30-second ads I do that keep the Gallery name in front of prospective customers. We want to be first in the minds of customers who are thinking about furniture. Remember, IBM didn't invent the computer, Sperry Rand did. However, IBM was the first computer company to build a familiar reference in the minds of people looking to buy a computer. This first position changed once Dell, Compaq, and Gateway entered the market.

The Gallery formula for positioning the company and what it stands for in the community is simplicity. Who can keep up with all the communications bombarding people from television, newspapers, radio, billboards, and the Internet? If you are going to make an impression on people, you have to do it quickly and on the first attempt. My "saves you money" tag line started years ago and is still weaved into Gallery promotions. Gallery cuts through the communication jam on the airwaves by keeping everything simple.

MACK SPEAK

Branding at Gallery

Keeping the Gallery Furniture brand name in the public's thoughts takes a lot of advertising and promotion. This is my contribution to Gallery. Being heard and seen is how the Gallery name became so recognized.

When Gallery fulfills requests for help, it keeps most of them private. We keep over 90 percent of the giving instances between the recipient and us.

ALWAYS PRESENT

By giving back to the community, delivering over 30,000 30-second commercials annually, wearing my logo-loaded golf shirts and hats, delivering over 300 speeches per year, buying the Houston Livestock Show and Rodeo grand champion steers, and using sports team promotions, we have kept the Gallery brand name in front of everyone in the region. We also live by the mottos of "delighting customers" and "same-day delivery." This is purposefully and carefully planned. The competition has to keep up with Gallery because we are at the head of the furniture-store-recognition scale. Competition is fierce and not always honest. Being dishonest is unacceptable at Gallery.

MACK LESSON

Delighting Customers Is Free

Philip Crosby said that superior quality in a product is free. At Gallery, providing service that delights customers is free. It doesn't cost a penny. It builds customer loyalty and makes our customers ambassadors because they tell everyone about the great services Gallery provided. Word-of-mouth publicity is fantastic.

Gallery was not the first furniture store on the north side of Houston. While it has become recognized and its brand name known, its position is continually being tested by competitors. One reason for our success is the employees. Another reason is that Gallery is involved in the community and keeps talking about who, where, and what the store offers. We make noise on purpose. The noise we make is frequent and with the same "saves you money" tag line.

Every school child is taught that Christopher Columbus discovered America in 1492. Unfortunately, he made the mistake of exploring and keeping his mouth shut. Guess what! The place where he landed was later named America after Amerigo Vespucci who traveled there a few years after Columbus did. Vespucci talked about the new land and created the story that it was part of a separate continent. He talked and wrote about the New World, and the Europeans credited him for the discovery of what they then called America, after his name. The lesson here is advertising coupled with giving back to the community can position your business brand in the minds of customers and prospective customers.

HOW TO BECOME A BRIGHT POINT OF LIGHT

Instead of describing points of light as primarily community groups only, it is my view that an individual business owner can be a powerful beacon of one.

It's easy to see the impact of Candy Lightner on so many people. She was a powerful influence and example of what persistence and working to help others really means in life-and-death terms. If you look at the work of Candy Lightner, you should notice some crucial personal attributes, namely, hard work, persistence, passion, a cause that is the focal point, and a sense of fulfillment in accomplishing something that is meaningful. Most of us can't possibly aspire to be such a force as Candy Lightner. However, anyone can accomplish some fantastic things by following a systematic program. While it would be easy to run out and volunteer for a host of charity work or community groups, don't be so anxious. If you are going to be in it for the long haul, take some time and follow a systematic approach. Volunteering or agreeing to serve on a committee that isn't right for you can quickly become a problem.

In my keep-it-simple-and-concise style, let me offer some point-of-light guidelines. The three hints that follow should be modified to fit your personality and style. Don't look for the perfect fit. Perfect is not going to pop up in most cases.

Organize the Choices

First, divide your opportunities to give and help others into categories. Such division could be children, faith-based organizations, community action groups, charities, neighborhoods, and open-end activities. You can find many contributions to make in any of these categories. Don't use this breakdown if you have your own way of dividing opportunities. You also may want to focus all of your attention on only one of these categories.

My focus is on children, neighborhoods, and open-end situations. It seems right for me at the time. It is likely that my preferences and needs will change a number of times in the next few years.

Your skills, preferences, needs, and goals will help direct you into a primary area or a select number of areas. If you conduct a thorough self-awareness check-up, where you end up will fit you properly.

The organizing step should be tied to your schedule. Do an honest time check. How much time can you devote to your selected areas? Be honest. It takes a lot of discipline to accurately determine the time you have to give. For example, if you select working with Big Brothers, make sure that you consider the time needed to be the very best Big Brother you can be. If you are going to serve meals at a homeless shelter, calculate the time needed to serve, to interact with people at the shelter, and to travel to and from the shelter. Build a complete list of time commitments.

Pause and Think

Second, pause and think. Now you have to become serious. Communities have entire databases and clearinghouses devoted to opportunities for giving and helping others. You can also talk with the publicly-known leaders of giving and helping in your town or neighborhood. These discussions and a careful review of clearinghouse materials will uncover situations that spark your interest. You will have many choices, so take your time to investigate thoroughly.

The opportunities to help and give may also be impromptu, such as the Houston flood of 2001 or the tragic terrorist attacks on the World Trade Center, the Pentagon, and the crashed plane in Pennsylvania on September 11, 2001. When disasters occur, many opportunities to help simply appear. Even in these cases, you need to pick out those activities to best fit your preferences, needs, and motivations. You will have to study in a faster time cycle the requests for help that appear soon after a disaster. At Gallery, we pick out a limited number of disaster-event requests for help. We can't possibly do everything that we are asked to do.

Narrow Down the Choices

Third, narrow your range. Whether you are considering ongoing opportunities or disaster-initiated situations, you must focus on only a few. Time, schedules, and resources are the limiting factors. If Gallery could, it would pick many more opportunities to give back and help others. It is best, however, to jump into only a few of the opportunities. In-depth work and help in a few areas results in more noticeable consequences than is the case when a large number of opportunities are seized.

To determine the few opportunities you will seize, conduct due-diligence investigations of the organizations you will give to and support. What are the organizations achieving? What are the goals of the organizations? Who is in charge? What is the financial status of each organization?

MACK CASE

A Lot of Choices to Consider

The choices a person can make for helping others is endless. A good starting list could include the following:

- *The place you were born, raised, went to school*
- *A school that made a difference*
- *A playground that you spent time on*
- *A neighborhood in need of help*
- *A cause that has touched you*
- *A family in need of immediate help*
- *The area around your business*
- *Scholarships*
- *Human service agencies such as the Salvation Army*

Johnny Carson, the late-night TV entertainer never forgot his hometown of Norfolk, Nebraska, and the community center in Logan, Iowa, where his grandparents lived. He made giving-back choices based on his family background. Because there are so many worthy causes, some thought must go into narrowing down the list.

Become Involved

Fourth, after answering the due-diligence questions and receiving satisfactory answers, become involved. You have to become involved in ongoing activities and volunteer for assignments. You have to be willing to start at the bottom and do what is necessary to show you are committed. Just as is true in branding, you must position yourself in the organization. Show that you are serious by becoming involved in the meetings, work sessions, and other necessary duties.

After becoming involved, track the organization's progress and activities. Ask for updated financial records, talk to the leaders, and talk to the recipients of the giving-and-help program. Do not rely on public relations reports informing the public of the organization's effectiveness. Find out firsthand what is being done.

Teach Others

Fifth, as you become involved, get others in your business and community engaged. Take the opportunity to teach others that giving back and caring are worthy endeavors. Teach others the value of being a point of light. Teach them that making life better for others produces one of the warmest feelings a person can experience.

At Gallery, we have created a culture that encourages and invites everyone to share in the giving-and-helping-others programs. Showing others that you care, are involved, and are serious communicates a message. Providing employees with the time to join in helping others is another message that teaches the value of what the business is doing. As a teacher, you can influence by serving as a role model, a powerful way to influence others.

MACK LESSON

Do Your Own Self-Awareness Check!

Do you know who you are in terms of giving to and helping others? Do you know what is important to you, and what opportunities you can impact by helping? Do a self-awareness check. Ask a few friends what they think about you? It may be surprising, and it may hurt. Be brave and take the plunge.

Identify your own community heroes and leaders. What are they doing and how are they doing it? Study their track record and accomplishments.

What are you now giving to your community? Who are you helping? How do you grade yourself on the giving and helping scale with "1" being zero involvement and "10" being a lot of giving and helping.

After taking stock by doing the self-awareness check, follow the five steps to become a point of light:

1. *Organize the choices.*
2. *Pause and think.*
3. *Narrow down the choices.*
4. *Become involved.*
5. *Teach others.*

10

Mack's Lessons

What lies behind us and what lies before us are small matters compared to what lies within us.

RALPH WALDO EMERSON

Each person has his or her own principles for accomplishing their important goals. The seven management and marketing principles I have presented need to be tailored for each person. My life journey and happiness are made possible by following these management and marketing guidelines, being fortunate or lucky, by spiritual forces beyond my ability to comprehend, hard work, friends, family, and mentors like W. Edwards Deming. Each person reading this book must carve out a personal program to begin the journey. Prepare your own personal principles to reach goals that are important to you.

Lessons learned during my work history have been important guideposts along my journey. Some of what I learned eventually became a habit because of repetitiveness. However, one person's habits can't do

211

much for another person, because they are unique to only you. "One More Time!" is just a quick reminder of the Mack Lessons introduced throughout the book.

One More Time!

- *Establish a values-based culture.*
- *Follow FAST: Focus, Action, Search, Tenacity.*
- *Direct your energy.*
- *Sell with pride and passion.*
- *Build and nurture relationships.*
- *Think Big in everything you do.*
- *Give back again and again.*

How you modify, execute, and review these principles to fit your style, personality, and needs is up to you. Building your own principles to be a better manager, friend, partner, spouse, or community leader is a personal matter. It will take a lot of commitment, hard work, and action.

LEAVING THE EXCUSE TRAIN

Starting your program requires action now. Don't get on the "excuse train." It starts with a little momentum and builds up steam. It starts with the typical excuses: "I'm traveling too much now, so I'll start my diet next month." "I could have done a better job if I had more time." "I was late because my dog was lost and I had to search for him." One excuse leads to another. Pretty soon you can fill a book up with excuse memos, notes, and stories.

If you closely study successful people, you'll find that they don't use excuses. They act, they do. President Harry Truman could have used the "I don't have a college education" excuse and not run for President. He refused to hide behind an excuse and achieved the highest political office in the United States.

No legitimate excuse exists to not improve yourself, your family life, or your community involvement. Don't waste your time making excuses or just dreaming about doing or taking action. You must produce success; it will not just appear. To succeed in selling furniture, Gallery employees have to make it happen. We had to earn the business and loyalty of customers. We started by opening the doors in 1981 and learning over the years what delights customers. Doing, experimenting, changing, and working hard were all part of the Gallery business approach.

The seven Mack principles are my guideposts for success. These principles have enabled me to do the following:

- Visualize and Dream
- Display Integrity
- Have Self-Confidence
- Display Confidence in People
- Develop Exceptional Listening Skills

VISUALIZE AND DREAM

Everyone wants to be something exceptional. My reading of a number of astronaut biographies taught me that they dreamed about the stars, galaxies, and about venturing one day into space in a starship. I wanted to be an NFL football star with the Dallas Cowboys. I watched and listened to their games. My dream was clear. I played ball at all levels through college. One day I woke up and realized that my dream wasn't going to happen.

I was able to pick up the pieces and talk to friends and family to help create a new set of dreams. My next dreams centered on being a successful businessperson. I dreamed about owning my own business. One day I dreamed about operating a health club. The next dream was about selling goods to people who were happy with me and my products. I kept refocusing my dream on different kinds of business. Furniture retailing occasionally popped up but not more often than most other business ideas.

Dreams can be powerful motivators for taking action. One employee at Gallery showed me how powerful dreams can be. Juan worked in the Gallery warehouse stacking furniture and moving it on and off the showroom floor. He approached me after about two years of warehouse work and asked about becoming a salesperson. To my surprise, he had always wanted to sell, but no one ever asked him. I asked him why he thought he could sell furniture. He said, "Because I know furniture, I like people, and I have dreamed about selling for years." Juan was a dreamer who wanted the opportunity to take action. We made him a salesperson, and he has been successful. Year after year for the last eight years he has been one of Gallery's top salespeople.

If Juan accepted his warehouse position as his permanent job, he would never have been given the opportunity to sell. He didn't accept being a warehouseman and kept his dream alive for the right moment. Gallery was fortunate in that he finally went after what he dreamed about and wanted.

Before you start to assemble your own plan and lessons to follow, think about what you want. If you are considering a job change, visualize the ideal job. Don't hold back. Let your big dream evolve. Most people have to learn how to dream again. When you were young, dreams were a natural process. Try to reestablish your ability to dream. Practice, practice, practice dreaming each day.

DISPLAY INTEGRITY

A person's word is sacred. A few years ago, one Wall Street wonderkin made a big stir when he said, "Greed is a good thing." It is not, and it was not for him personally. After making the statement, he was found guilty and sent to jail for unethical practices. Integrity is one of the most significant predictors of business success. It is the cornerstone of doing business with others. If customers can't trust a business or its representatives, they will take their business elsewhere. Building Gallery on a foundation of keeping promises, selling with pride, and focusing on customer delight is how the business succeeded. We thrive on hearing from customers that Gallery treats people with integrity.

You must pay attention to everything you promise. Being honest, truthful, and fair are not flexible or bendable principles. A white lie or false promise is still a blow to your integrity armor. Stealing is stealing even if it is a piece of fruit in a grocery store or $1 million worth of stock. Any deviation from integrity chips away at your foundation of values. Deviations are probably going to occur simply because zero defects are impossible with human beings. We all have slight integrity flaws and setbacks.

Try this little integrity quiz in the following Mack Lesson to see where you currently stand. These eight questions test your integrity, and you should ask them periodically. Answering them honestly measures your integrity, and sometimes you will not like the result. When I'm hitting on all cylinders, my integrity score and feelings are good. When a person is viewed as possessing integrity, he or she is trusted by others.

MACK LESSON

An Integrity Quiz

Answer the following questions to learn about your integrity. Be honest, and you can learn a lot about who you really are.

1. How well do you treat people from whom you gain nothing?

2. *Are you the same person with everyone you deal with, playing no particular favorites?*

3. *Do you easily admit wrongdoing or admit making a mistake without being asked or pressed?*

4. *Do you gossip about someone's flaws or deficiencies, or do you talk to the person directly about them?*

5. *Do you have strict moral principles that do not bend?*

6. *Do you regularly tell white lies to get out of tight spots or situations?*

7. *Do you pass the buck by blaming others for errors or oversights you committed?*

8. *Do you keep every promise you make?*

Trust in someone or in a company is rare in the business world. However, without trust a business is in serious trouble. Trust creates customer loyalty. Time and time again in talking to repeat customers at Gallery it is made clear to me that trust is what brings them back. They trust the Gallery brand, service, and products. Again and again the promise of same-day delivery is brought up by customers. Gallery employees try to never promise anything that we can't deliver.

By earning customers' trust, Gallery is able to gain their business. The power of trust and confidence in building loyal customers should be at the top of any business's must-do list. By being committed to keeping every promise, the integrity of each Gallery representative is solidified. Violations of integrity are not tolerated at Gallery. If any employee deals dishonestly or makes false promises, he or she will be immediately disciplined.

Integrity Is the Gold Standard

Nothing is a substitute for integrity. It's the ultimate characteristic of any man or woman. Remember the following:

- *Always be honest with the customer. You must manage each customer's experience.*
- *Don't tell a customer to call another department. Solve the problem by not passing the buck.*
- *Don't promise anything special that you yourself can't make happen.*
- *Don't present the product you're selling as anything but what it is.*

HAVE SELF-CONFIDENCE IN YOURSELF

If you become successful, you will have some scar tissue from the arrows shot at you. Becoming confident in who and what you are means you will have to fight off fear. Fear is ready to consume you when you take a risk, try something new, or make a major decision. People are fearful of failing, of looking like a fool.

There are many types of fear, including fear of being rejected, public speaking, flying, conflict, lack of knowledge, technology, the future, and success. Each of these common fears can stop you dead in your tracks. Confidence in yourself will be needed to overcome these and other fears.

Be Firm and Fair

Gallery terminates employees for stealing, lying, or being dishonest in dealing with customers. You can't bend your integrity standards if you want to gain the trust and confidence of others. Committing yourself to being a truthful, honest, and hard-working person should become a habit. It will become a habit when you practice it every single day, in every situation.

A confident person can combat fears by taking action. Confidence grows by doing, by stretching oneself. Only action can result in more confidence. Remember, making excuses is not acceptable. You have to take charge.

Confidence to succeed by taking action is displayed by professional athletes. Gallery has sponsored many sporting events, and this has allowed Gallery employees to see athletes up close as they compete. One of the best examples of personal confidence was displayed by Hakeem Olajuwon when he played for the Houston Rockets. Hakeem in the 1993-1994 and 1994-1995 seasons carried the team to the NBA Championship. He was totally confident in his talent and skill. He projected this confidence on the court and in the locker room. Olajuwon's demeanor was one of confidence. The result was two world championships, the only ones in the Rockets' history.

There are a number of confidence strength-building exercises you can use. First, you can read about successful people in books, articles, and magazines. Stories of recovering from failure and reaching a seemingly impossible goal are especially rewarding.

Surround yourself with positive people. Positive words, examples, and behaviors are powerful signals that anything can be accomplished. Remember that you need to avoid the can't-do people. Run with the positive people, and it will shape, motivate, and inspire your own behavior.

Reward yourself for the good things you do. If you help others and give back to those who are less fortunate, be humble but also be proud. If your new sales program takes off, celebrate the success. Don't be a naysayer about good accomplishments. You don't need to advertise your accomplishments, but, at a minimum, tell yourself you helped make a difference. You have to believe in your own accomplishments before you can be a natural helper of others.

DISPLAY CONFIDENCE IN PEOPLE

People you work with need to be cared for in terms of recognition, trust, and confidence. If you can clearly show confidence in another person, he or she will want to work as hard as possible to not disappoint you.

Great leaders show by their actions that they have confidence in their followers.

Showing confidence can be displayed by letting people do their assignment, work, project, or job with the best resources but with limited close supervision. Most people want some structure and direction, but they want freedom more. There is a delicate line where too much direction and firsthand supervision becomes too restrictive and stifling. People will flourish when they are confident that you trust them enough to do a good job. If you set up an atmosphere of trust, fairness, high integrity, and personal development, you will improve the person's sense of belonging and teamwork.

Years ago, one of my professor friends told me to spare the criticism and monitoring and lavish the recognition. He kept telling me to reign in my tendency, at the time, to oversee everything. As Gallery grew, he warned me, my desire to see, hear, and critique everything would be impossible to achieve. He was right on target. But recognizing outstanding accomplishments, such as delivering furniture in a driving rainstorm, helping a customer make a difficult choice, or accommodating a handicapped customer's needs, is possible and worth my time and energy. When someone is recognized, he or she feels great.

My confidence-building recipe is easy to use. It starts with being positive and encouraging everyone to do his or her best. Letting people have breathing room in the amounts they prefer is my common practice. Next, I recognize again and again exceptional displays of keeping promises, providing same-day delivery, and delighting customers. I am always on the lookout for exceptional moments of integrity, sensitivity, good-will, happiness and fun, and appreciation. At Gallery, we create an atmosphere that applauds being a part of a team. We like each other and help each other. Displaying confidence in others on the team is done by example. It becomes a habit and is rather easy to do after only a brief time.

MACK CASE

Taking Care of Customers at Nordstrom

Gallery has learned from other companies like Nordstrom, Disney, and Lands' End. Every new employee at Nordstrom receives the following brief statement of welcome:

We're glad to have you with our company.

Our number one goal is to provide outstanding customer service.

Set both your personal and professional goals high.

We have great confidence in your ability to achieve them.

Nordstrom Rules:

Rule #1: Use your good judgment in all situations.

There will be no additional rules. Please feel free to ask your department manager, store manager, or division manager any question at any time.

Sometimes, clearly displaying confidence in others takes some time. Don't be discouraged. Each person has their own internal counter or sensor for determining when they are appreciated or feel like a part of an important team. These sensors work differently in each of us. Be accessible, listen carefully, keep the negatives out of your vocabulary, and show people you believe in them. The rewards in return will be powerful. People do not want to disappoint friends, colleagues, or managers whom they respect. I can't explain what goes on inside the person, but I've seen the benefits of having confidence in others—working harder, being proud, being loyal and trusting, helping others, and supporting the mission of Gallery.

DEVELOP EXCEPTIONAL LISTENING SKILLS

It took me years to button up my mouth and use my ears more. My early style was to talk at people and not hang around too long to hear their responses. What my style cost me was a reputation of being only a talker. When you listen to someone, it sends a powerful message that the person is important. People are impressed when another person shows respect by listening. You also learn a lot by listening.

In my business, customers have a lot to say about prices, quality, service, the merchandise Gallery sells, and store layout. It's amazing how much we learn from our customers. Because we don't know what customers want or are thinking, it is important to listen to them. My listening extends from customers to employees, competitors, experts, and even leaders from other industries. You can learn, get ideas, and solve problems better if you have the ability to listen.

In order to be an exceptional listener, you have to work hard at it. Talking is easier than listening. Most people practice long and hard to be a great verbal communicator. The image of the great verbal communicators, such as Abraham Lincoln, John F. Kennedy, Martin Luther King, Jr., and Winston Churchill, is centered on talking, presenting, and persuading others through inspirational words. The listening part of these great orators' talents is never mentioned even though they were all known to be great listeners.

MACK LESSON

Customer Rules

- *Acknowledge customers as you walk through the store.* **Smile, be happy.**
- *Create customer excitement about their new purchase. You need to compliment them for the decision to give Gallery their business.* **Feel good.**
- *Make your customers feel good—start by listening to them.* **Don't interrupt.**

The truth of the matter is that exceptional listening requires you to focus and expend energy. Turning off your own words to focus, as explained in Chapter 4, is difficult. You will need discipline and energy to focus on what others are saying.

Listening is such a vital part of doing business that having to work at it seems exhausting. It is, and it takes practice. By practicing, listening will become a habit. My own approach to listening follows the simple pattern shown in the Mack Lesson below.

Four To-Do Actions for Listening

1. *Allow the other person the time to speak.*

2. *Make eye contact and focus on the other person's eyes.*

3. *Don't interrupt. This has been and is one of my toughest things to do. I'm a "red personality" who thrives on action. Not to interrupt is tough for me to do. The next time you are interacting with someone, try to count the times you interrupt.*

4. *Do not prejudge or stereotype the speaker. When you prejudge, you fail to pick up what is being said. Leave the stereotyping to someone else. A salesperson who prejudges because of the appearance or speaking ability of the potential customer can and usually does lose the sale.*

Trust, confidence, and loyalty are shown by listening with focus and energy. Good listeners seem to attract friends, partners, customers, and people in general. Everyone wants to have someone listen to him or her. If you become a good listener, you have found another way to give two important things to the other person—time and attention. Good listeners build up loyal fans, and this is an important benefit in business. Loyal fans stay and become loyal customers.

DEVELOP YOUR PERSONAL PLAN

To awaken your potential, you have to prepare in your mind, on paper, or through self-talk your own personal plan. In a nutshell, you have to lead yourself to success. Now is the time to review the Mack Lessons explained in this book and to think about how you can incorporate them into your personal plan.

Values-Based Culture

To build a values-based culture, you are going to have to monitor yourself on integrity and on personal dreams. Do you still dream? About what? Are you honest? If you don't like your answers, do something about it. Excuses are not acceptable. The promises made, promises kept lesson sets a valuable standard that guides me personally and drives Gallery Furniture. It is the rock-solid foundation of everything we do. Being zero defects on every promise is probably impossible. Just because we haven't been perfect doesn't diminish the power of this lesson. Keep this lesson as close to 100 percent perfect as possible.

FAST

It has taken me years to be able to focus with intensity on top priority goals. After years of practice, I focus on people, problems, goals, and what people are saying. This intensity sometimes is exhausting. It is worth it because my relationships with employees, customers, my family, and the community are deeper and more rewarding because of it. As I have said before, success doesn't come to you. You go get it. Focus doesn't simply occur. You have to work at it in every interaction. I am energized because of my focus. Living only on dreams and visualization is not enough. You need to focus, act, search, all with tenacity, FAST. Remember, no excuses!

Action before Energy

You need to get moving, taking action so that energy is produced. Start by focusing so you can see more, hear more, and think more, which are all valuable providers of knowledge and insight. You are able to examine your own strengths and weaknesses which helps you improve. Focusing is an action that requires a lot of energy, time, patience, and skill. Monitoring your actions, not being distracted by negative events or messages, and being positive are all focused behaviors.

Sell with Pride

Everyone is a salesperson in life. You may not have a title or be called a salesperson, but you are always selling. People sell themselves. Why not do it with integrity, confidence, and professionalism? Instead of denying that we are all selling something, focus on becoming the best salesperson possible. Tom Peters hit it on the head when he proposed that "brand you" needs to be nurtured, packaged, promoted, and renewed occasionally. Understanding this is difficult for most people. We have been taught to be humble about our skills, abilities, and talents, but this has been carried too far. Being a braggart and a bag of self-promotion is not what Peters is suggesting. Knowing who you are and selling these skills, abilities, and talents professionally is necessary so that goals are accomplished.

In building your own program, leave some time and resources for yourself, for taking care of your needs, replenishing your energy, and rewarding yourself for good work or for being a bright point of light. Being honest about yourself is good and healthy. If you feel good about yourself, you will find you have always-new and vibrant energy to help others. This in turn results in others having more trust and confidence in you, which means that people want to be in your good graces and network.

Selling yourself, your business, and your ideas with pride is a significant way to attract others. People are attracted to confident, visionary, and inspiring individuals. The relationships that result can be another boost to keeping promises, giving back to others, and Thinking Big. Everyone needs relationships. If you are able to sell yourself, you not only have meaningful relationships, but you also have eager helpers. Having a diverse relationship team is a key to successfully operating a business.

Selling Starts with Confidence

People have to believe in themselves in order to sell themselves to others. Without confidence we waiver, when we should be selling and taking pride in our accomplishments. Talk to yourself and know who you are. Focus on all the value you add to a business, to a situation, to a problem that needs to be solved. Others may attempt to take you off your game. Don't permit anyone to stop you from selling who and what you are.

Building Relationships

The one skill that goes a long way in building deep and loyal relationships is to listen intensely. Everyone wants to be heard, especially people who trust you with personal information, thoughts, and ideas. Set aside time to practice how to listen until it becomes a habit. It will probably take a lot of practice. Fight against the tendency to put listening at the bottom of your to-do list. Because relationships will be at the core of any success you enjoy, you need to work at their development.

Think Big!

The principle of Thinking Big should be another part of your personal plan. We have become a nation of calorie counters. If you eat too many calories and don't exercise, you will gain weight. If you believe that your body is what it is fed, so is your mind. If your mind only thinks small or is uncertain, then you will act accordingly. In addition to doing the necessary small things, you should also Think Big and Think Bold. Telling me that it was impossible to adhere to my promise of same-day delivery was like a jump start to me. Instead of accepting the naysayers' views about furniture delivery, I made up my mind to prove the doubters wrong. I never doubted that Gallery could be the business that brings same-day delivery into the furniture industry. I refused to accept the noise coming at me for being "foolish," a "huckster," and a "crazy dreamer."

Surrendering to the doubters and the naysayers would have been easy. Surrendering or changing my big dream was never an option. The pessimistic, negative, can't-do-it thinking of others required me to focus, pay attention to details, and to work around the clock. To me, pessimism, small thinking, and ridicule are poisons to be avoided.

Thinking Big in the furniture business means taking care of customers first. Everything Gallery has done, from expanding the size of the store to helping flood victims, to purchasing Elvis's convertible, to sponsoring the Men's U.S. Clay Court Tennis Championship, and to purchasing the grand champion steers at the rodeo has started with Thinking Big. The drive to do things and give back to my community is delighting customers. Putting customer delight in the spotlight requires doing everything we do first class.

The size of Gallery's success is based on the big goals that we set. Whether you are ever successful at school, at work, at home, or wherever, will be a matter of your personal action. Why think small? Just Think Big, work hard, learn, and sacrifice. People who reach the top in acting, music, sports, business, medicine, or any profession get there with their own personal plan, and a lot of effort. Why not go for Big?

Think of three goals that you want to accomplish in the next six months. Take a few minutes. Then write them down in the Mack Lesson, "Your Personal Big Goals."

MACK LESSON

Your Personal Big Goals

1. _____

_____

_____

2. _____

_____

_____

3. _____

_____

_____

Are any of the goals you listed routine goals, or are they all big, stretching, meaningful goals? Set high, big, and bold goals. Keep focused on big goals, don't procrastinate, and exert energy to accomplish them. Big Thinking and Big Goals can lead to Big Success. Don't sell yourself short by focusing on nonstretch, trivial goals. You are in charge of pushing the envelope and stretching who you are.

Acting Philanthropically

Thinking Big will allow you to feel the power of accomplishment. The impact of being successful can be personal, organizational, and community-wide. The community-wide impact of being financially, organizationally, and/or personally able to help others is now one of my most inspiring, rewarding experiences. As you recall, I informed you that giving back to others was not one of my early characteristics. I dabbled in a random and unfocused way in giving back by purchasing turkeys for Thanksgiving dinner at a homeless shelter or helping out someone with a few dollars. After becoming successful in a big way, Gallery has ratcheted up its community giving and involvement.

Gallery is not able to do everything requested, but we are proud and willing to do big things for Houston flood victims, ill and elderly citizens, needy children, and charities. By being successful, we are able to do many worthwhile things for others. Thinking Big and Succeeding Big has inspired Gallery to become a bright point of light. We are proud of our capability to help others. Yes, it has meant more customers, more positive publicity, and more goodwill. These are benefits that Gallery enjoys. You can be a beneficiary of thinking and accomplishing big things if you start with a positive mindset. Putting customer delight first worked for Gallery. You have to find your own big goals and stick with them through all the sniping and naysaying.

WHAT IS SUCCESS?

Success is such a fuzzy word that it's hard to reach agreement on its definition. I have tried to say in this book that success is in the eye of the beholder. The mix of ingredients that go into success varies a great deal from person to person. I define success as being able to delight my customers. It's my view that profits, growth, and gratification flow from delighting Gallery customers.

Delighting customers is the key to all my success. By delighting them through providing value, being positive and friendly, listening, helping solve their problems, and exceeding their expectations, I have experienced over and over again phenomenal consequences: goodwill, repeat business out of loyalty, converting a happy customer into a salesperson for Gallery, and outselling competitors who are unable to deliver the goods the same day. I instill this kind of delight-the-customer thinking in every Gallery employee. Gallery employees are just like our customers; we only want to hear the words, "Sure, we can do that."

In order to continually delight customers, you must gain and earn their loyalty. It is not enough to just satisfy customers. Businesses must earn their customer's loyalty. When you are fair, honest, sincere, entertaining, focused, and a good listener, you earn customer loyalty.

In any business, breaking promises results in annoyed, frustrated, and irritated customers. Eventually, these emotions build up and the customer leaves. Customers who have negative experiences tell others. One of your major management challenges is to instill the importance of not breaking promises in every person you manage. This will have to be done through example after example. As the manager, you are the role model. Others watch every move you make, listen to every word you utter, and imitate your actions.

Customers have expectations about their interactions with your business. By exceeding these expectations, your business can become and remain attractive to customers, building a case of customer examples that illustrate why loyalty is good.

Customer delight results from not only meeting but exceeding customer expectations. Pleasant and unexpected surprises create customer delight. For example, a middle-aged couple visited Gallery after returning from an overseas work assignment. They were very concerned that their existing motorized beds needed to fit within the frame of the king-size headboard, footboard, and rails they wanted to purchase. The Gallery Furniture salesperson, Jack, listened very carefully to their description of the problem and their concerns. He thought about the task and said, "We can do the job, if you give us a chance." Jack and his crew delivered over $20,000 worth of furniture and then started on the bed project. The crew worked for hours constructing a wooden platform upon which the motorized bed would rest.

The completed project was a masterpiece of workmanship because everything fit perfectly. The arrangement looked like it was custom-made, as it was. The customers were excited and pleased. The work and care of Jack's crew exceeded their expectations. They had all their furniture the same day they bought it, and the motorized bed problem was solved. We earned their business, respect, and future furniture purchases.

Gallery can only focus on or increase customer delight by listening, collecting information, and being observant. After years of experience in listening to and observing customer expectations, it becomes easier. Never perfect, but a lot easier. What is tricky is that the better Gallery gets, the higher the customers' expectations become. If we delivered furniture five hours after the purchase on one occasion, the next time the customer expects only a three-hour gap between purchase and delivery. Customers ratchet up their expectations. It is a natural process of escalation.

As you know, my customer-delight approach starts with customers as people. Yes, I want them to buy the furniture they need, but I want to know them first. Gallery sells more furniture to the people we know personally. Taking the time to learn about people builds their self-esteem. A person's overall feeling of self-worth is very important in selling any product or service. The better customers feel about themselves, the more delighted they become. People who feel good buy more.

Nordstrom and Disney are masters at making customers feel good. Disney's theme parks are designed so well that moms and dads always look like brilliant and wonderful parents in the eyes of their happy children. Parents feel good that they can provide their children a nice wholesome experience. Kids plead with parents to take them back to Disney World. Disney exceeds customer expectations in entertainment, safety, cleanliness, and variety. We imitate these four Disney characteristics at Gallery Furniture: We entertain, provide safe and secure childcare areas, keep an immaculate store, and offer a wide variety of furniture. We learned from the experts like Nordstrom and Disney how to meet and exceed customer expectations.

Learning from others like Nordstrom and Disney takes patience, time away from Gallery to observe how other businesses work, and focusing on improving strengths and correcting weaknesses. Keeping promises, Thinking Big, and building strong relationships all require work.

After reading this book, you are probably anxious to get started on your own program. Here are a few "must dos," no matter what approach you take to improve or better yourself.

- Develop a vision. Paint a picture of what you want and don't let naysayers take you off course.
- Understand people and respect a wide range of differences.

- Work hard. Don't underestimate how hard you are going to have to work to be successful, however you define success.
- Keep it simple. We are all bombarded by an overwhelming volume of noise, fact, and information. Whatever you do, keep it simple.
- Have courage. Changing, making tough decisions, starting a project all require courage. You must work on having the self-confidence to stand up and do something.

You can practice and train yourself to become a successful person. You are free to make decisions, to be in control of the journey you take. If you want delighted customers who will be loyal and create word-of-mouth advertising that says your business or service exceeds all expectations, you need to personalize the seven management and marketing principles in this book.

You now have a tough set of decisions facing you. First, you have to decide to make some changes. Are you ready? Second, you must visualize and dream about where you want to go. Are you ready? Third, you have to establish your own guidelines or lessons. That is, what lessons will you stick with and use? Are you ready? Fourth, you are going to have to check up periodically on how you are doing. If you find that you are backsliding, procrastinating, or making excuses, you need to take immediate action. Are you ready? Fifth, you are going to have to work harder than ever to have a chance at success. Following any plan can't promise success. Many readers will probably quit because it is hard work. For those who stick with developing their own lessons and work harder than ever, the results will be astonishing. Are you ready? Finally, whatever you do—Think Big. Don't ever underestimate what you can accomplish at work, for your family, and in life.

FINAL MACK LESSON

Always Think Big!

I have always enjoyed Thinking Big. The following statement from John Wesley says it much better than I ever could:

Do all the good you can,
By all the means you can,
In all the ways you can,
At all the times you can,
To all the people you can,
As long as you can.

INDEX

Share the message!

Bulk discounts
Discounts start at only 10 copies. Save up to 55% off retail price.

Custom publishing
Private label a cover with your organization's name and logo. Or, tailor information to your needs with a custom pamphlet that highlights specific chapters.

Ancillaries
Workshop outlines, videos, and other products are available on select titles.

Dynamic speakers
Engaging authors are available to share their expertise and insight at your event.

**Call Dearborn Trade Special Sales at 1-800-245-BOOK (2665)
or e-mail trade@dearborn.com**

Dearborn™
Trade Publishing
A **Kaplan Professional** Company